Great Handkerchief Tricks

Bruce Smith

Sterling Publishing Co., Inc.
New York

Editor: Shona Grimbley
Consultant Magicians: Anthony Owen and Marc Paul
Designer: Graham Curd at wda
Illustrator: Colin Woodman

Library of Congress Cataloging in Publication Data Available

10 9 8 7 6 5 4 3 2 1

Published by Sterling Publishing Company, Inc.
387 Park Avenue South New York, NY 10016
First Published partially in Great Britain
under the title *Handkercheif Tricks*
© 1995 Arcturus Publishing Limited/ Bruce Smith
Distributed in Canada by Sterling Publishing
C/o Canada Manda Group, One Atlantic Ave, Suite 105, Toronto, Ontario,
Canada M6K 3

ISBN 0-8069-7179-7

Contents

R0175081771

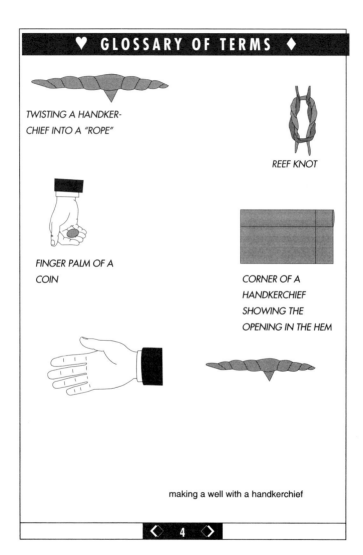

TWISTING A HANDKER-
CHIEF INTO A "ROPE"

REEF KNOT

FINGER PALM OF A
COIN

CORNER OF A
HANDKERCHIEF
SHOWING THE
OPENING IN THE HEM

making a well with a handkerchief

VANISHES

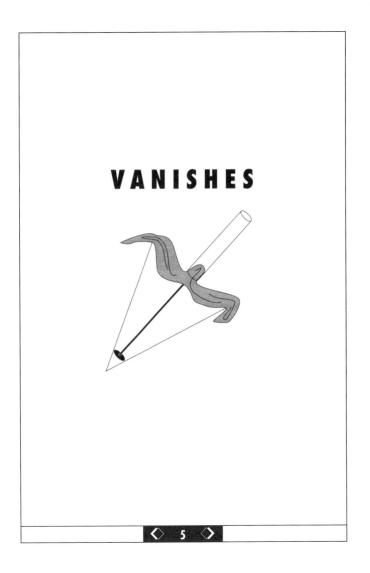

Effect *The magician ties a knot in the center of a silk handkerchief. When the spectators blow on the knot it simply melts away.*

Requirements *A silk handkerchief or scarf 45 x 45cm/18 x 18in.*

Preparation *None.*

• • • • • • • • • • • • • • • •

1 Hold the handkerchief by diagonally opposite corners between the first and second fingers of the left hand (end A) and the right hand (end B). Twist the handkerchief into a "rope" as shown in illustration 1.

2 Bring end B over to your left hand, passing it between your left second and third fingers, and clip end B under the left thumb (illustration 2).

3 Your right hand now goes through the loop and takes hold of end A. Your left third and fourth fingers hold down the silk "rope" below end A (illustration 3).

4 After the left third and fourth fingers close around the

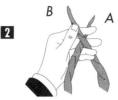

2

handkerchief, the left second finger clips the silk where the two ends cross (illustration 3).

5 Pull end A through the loop with your right hand. End B is held tightly between the left thumb and first finger. The left third and fourth fingers release their grip around the silk as your left second finger hooks and pulls the lower portion of end B through the loop (illustration 4).

6 As you pull on end A a knot will form around the loop held by the second finger of the left hand. Remove your left second finger from inside the loop when the knot is tight enough to hold its own shape. This appears to be a genuine knot, but it is actually a slip knot.

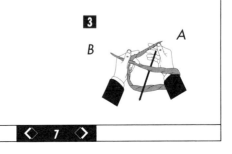

3

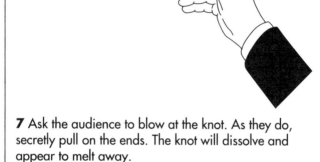

4

B

Pull

A

7 Ask the audience to blow at the knot. As they do, secretly pull on the ends. The knot will dissolve and appear to melt away.

ADE DUVAL (1898-1965)

Many magicians use silk handkerchief in their performances, but the American magician Ade Duval was one the few to create an entire act of "Silken Sorcery." With this unique act he travelled the world performing in exclusive glamourous night spots.

Effect *The magician pushes a silk handkerchief into his closed fist. After a suitable mystical pass the magician slowly opens his fist to show that the handkerchief has vanished!*

Requirements *A small hollow ball (a table tennis ball is ideal), a length of cord elastic, a safety pin and a silk handkerchief.*

Preparation *You will need to make a special prop known as a "pull." Cut a hole in one side of the ball large enough for the handkerchief to be pushed inside. Attach the ball to one end of the elastic and attach the safety pin to the other end (illustration 1). Pin the safety pin on the inside left of your jacket (illustration 2).*

1

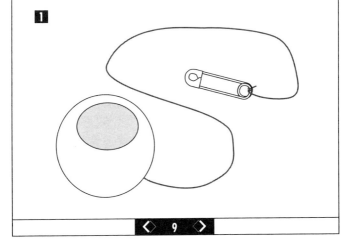

You will have to adjust the length of the cord elastic so that when it is stretched, the ball can be held comfortably in your right hand. When you release the ball the elastic should pull it up into your jacket. You need to experiment to get the right length of elastic for you.

Prepare by pinning the elastic inside your jacket as already described, and stretching the elastic so that you can hold the ball concealed in your closed right hand with the opening at the top (illustration 2) .

● ● ● ● ● ● ● ● ● ● ● ● ● ● ● ●

2

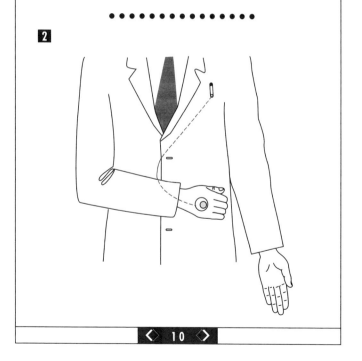

1 Display the handkerchief and push it inside your closed fist, ensuring it goes inside the ball (illustration 3).

2 Wave your empty hand over your closed fist, at the same time releasing the ball, allowing it to shoot quickly inside your jacket, taking the handkerchief with it.

3 After a sufficient build-up you can slowly open your hand to show that it is completely empty.

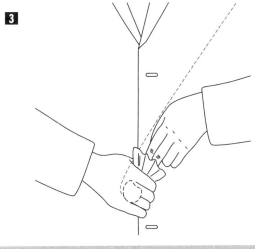

TOP TIPS FOR TRICKSTERS

Magic with colored silk handkerchiefs is ideal for entertaining young children because it is bright, bold and uses a prop which they can all relate to.

Effect *A coin, ring or card is wrapped in a handkerchief and then vanishes!*

Requirements *Two identical pocket handkerchiefs, preferably with a colorful pattern or design.*

Preparation *The two handkerchiefs are made into a special "vanishing" handkerchief. This type of prop is known among magicians as a utility prop, because it is a specially made item that can be used for many different effects.*

Sew the handkerchiefs together along the four edges, leaving the hem open at one corner (point A in illustration 1). This opening should be slightly bigger than the object you intend to vanish. Then sew the handkerchiefs together to form a V-shaped pocket inside the handkerchiefs (illustration 2). The point of the V should be just below the middle of the handkerchiefs so that the object inside will naturally fall to the middle.

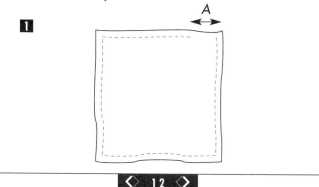

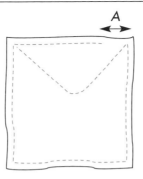

To give you an example of how to use the vanisher we will assume you want to vanish a borrowed coin. Prepare by inserting a duplicate of the coin you intend to use inside the secret pocket (illustration 3).

● ● ● ● ● ● ● ● ● ● ● ● ● ● ● ●

1 Hold the handkerchief by the corners at the top of the sewn V (due to the nature of the material the audience will be unable to see where it has been sewn). Drape the handkerchief over your open empty left palm so that the hidden coin rests on your hand.

2 Borrow a coin and place it directly on top of the secret hidden coin.

3 With your right hand pick up both coins together – the borrowed one and, through the layer of material, the hidden coin. Turn everything upside down so that the handkerchief covers the coins and your hand. Hang on to

3

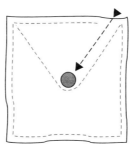

the hidden coin and allow the borrowed coin to slip into the palm of your hand where you can keep it concealed.

4 Ask a member of the audience to hold the coin through the handkerchief. They will feel the coin inside the handkerchief and hold it believing it to be the borrowed coin. When they have taken hold of the handkerchief and coin, allow your right hand to drop naturally to your side with the borrowed coin concealed in your curled fingers. You can secretly dispose of it in your pocket or load it somewhere to be reproduced later.

5 To vanish the coin hold one corner of the handkerchief and pull it from the spectator's grasp. They will feel the coin being pulled from their fingers, but fail to see it fall. It looks as though the coin has magically vanished in mid-air!

This is a very effective vanish and can be used in many other effects.

Effect *The magician makes a cone out of newspaper and pushes a silk handkerchief inside with a magic wand. The magician tears the newspaper into pieces to show that the silk handkerchief has completely vanished!*

Requirements *A newspaper, a silk handkerchief and a special magic wand (see "Preparation").*

Preparation *As the title of the effect suggests, it is the magic wand which makes the handkerchief disappear. To make this you will need a long thin hollow tube, plus a length of thin dowelling. Glue a circle of black card slightly larger than the diameter of the tube to the end of the dowelling (see illustration 1). Paint the tube black and white so that it looks like a magic wand.*

• • • • • • • • • • • • • • • •

1

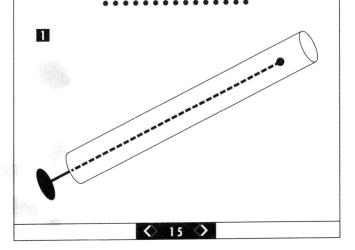

1 Form the newspaper into a cone. Rattle the magic wand inside the cone to prove it is empty. Secretly allow the rod to slide out and remain inside the cone. Drape the handkerchief over the mouth of the cone.

2 Using the magic wand you appear to push the silk down into the cone. In reality the wand slides over the rod and the rod and handkerchief are pushed up inside the hollow wand.

3 Remove the wand from the cone (with the rod and handkerchief tucked inside it) and set the wand down to one side.

5 Say the magic words and tear open the newspaper cone to show that it is completely empty!

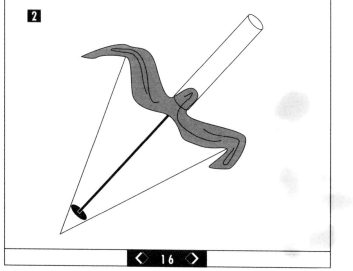

ANIMATION

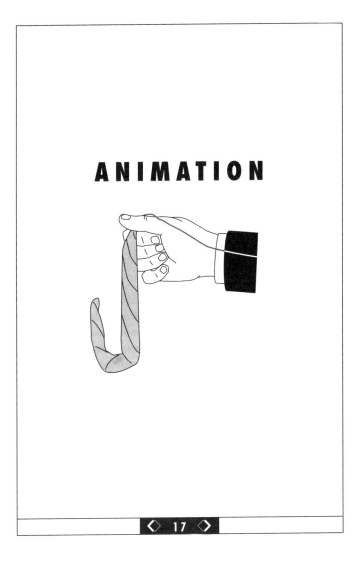

Effect *The magician hypnotizes a handkerchief and it moves mysteriously as though obeying commands.*

Requirements *A pocket handkerchief.*

Preparation *None.*

● ● ● ● ● ● ● ● ● ● ● ● ● ● ● ●

1 Claim to be able to hypnotize any pocket handkerchief. This is an impressive and unusual claim and will surely gain you the interest of your audience. Explain that you need to borrow somebody's handkerchief to be "put into a trance."

1

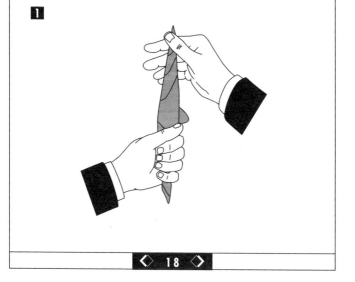

2 When you have borrowed a handkerchief spread it out flat on the table (it is always worth having a handkerchief of your own in your pocket in case nobody in your audience has one in a suitable state!).

3 Grab the top lefthand corner of the handkerchief with your left fingers and thumb, and with your right fingers and thumb hold the left edge about halfway down. Lift up the handkerchief and twist it between your hands to form a tightly twisted "rope."

4 Hold the handkerchief up vertically with your right hand at the top and the left hand below (illustration 1).

5 Keep hold with the right hand and move your left hand to a position about halfway up. As you do this make sure the handkerchief remains tightly twisted.

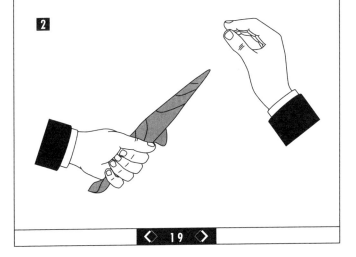

6 Pull the handkerchief tight between your hands and slowly let go with your right hand. The handkerchief will remain rigid as though hypnotized. "There you are," you say, "completely under my control!"

7 Gaze at the handkerchief and say in your most commanding tones, "Forward, forward, forward!" At the same time gently move your left thumb down the handkerchief and it will lean towards you.

8 Continue, "Back, back, back!" and move your left thumb back up the handkerchief. It will gradually slowly move away from you.

9 Repeat this a number of times, then move your left hand to hold the handkerchief horizontal to show it is rigid and completely in a trance. Say, "But it can be woken. On the count of three, when I snap my fingers it will wake up and will be unable to remember any of the things that have happened in the last few minutes!"

10 Return the handkerchief to its vertical position, click your fingers and flick open the handkerchief. Return it to its owner with a warning that it may never be the same again!

TOP TIPS FOR TRICKSTERS

Magic with silk handkerchiefs is often best when performed "silently" to a musical background, without the usual magician's patter.

This is not a baffling trick, but an amusing "bit of business" to perform either between tricks or to entertain a group of children at a social event. It would be a nice follow up to the "Hypnotized Hanky".

Effect *The magician transforms a pocket handkerchief into a doll-like replica of a ballet dancer. At the magician's command the figure seems to come alive with a high kicking spinning flourish!*

Requirements *A pocket handkerchief.*

Preparation *None.*

• • • • • • • • • • • • • • • •

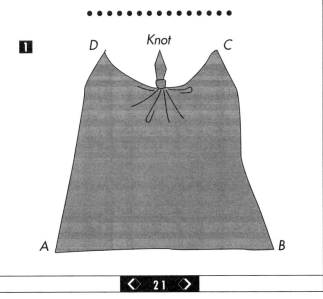

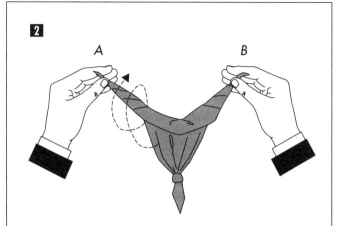

1 Lay the handkerchief on a flat surface and tie a knot halfway along one edge, leaving a "tail"' sticking out of the top of the knot to hold on to (illustration 1).

2 Hold the two corners of the bottom edge, opposite the edge with the knot in it. Twirl the handkerchief away from you (illustration 2). The weight of the knot will spin the handkerchief around the hem between your hands. Keep twisting the handkerchief tightly, until it cannot be twisted any further.

3 Bring the two corners in your hands together and grab them both in your right hand. With your left hand hold on to the "tail" sticking out of the knot. Turn everything around – with the knot at the top – so that it resembles a ballet dancer (illustration 3).

4 By moving your hands you can animate the "ballet dancer" so that she swings her hips or bows. If you let go of one corner with the right hand you can make her perform a high kick (illustration 4), and then go into a dramatic spin, until you are just left with a hanky with a knot in it! A ballet dancer's career is always short!

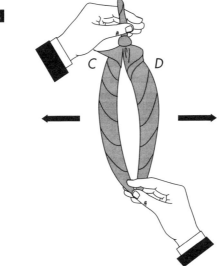

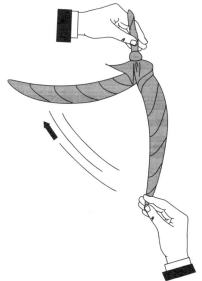

HOUDIN AND THE KING'S HANKIES

During Robert Houdin's Command performance at the palace of King Louis Phillipe he borrowed six handkerchiefs. The King requested that they should be magically sent under the last orange tree outside the palace. A guard was sent to the tree while Houdin vanished the bundle of hankies. An iron box was found buried under the selected tree and locked inside were the six borrowed handkerchiefs!

Effect *The magician ties a knot in the middle of a handkerchief. The handkerchief begins to move like a snake and unties the knot!*

Requirements *A silk handkerchief 45 x 45cm/18 x18in and 180cm/6ft of fine black nylon thread .*

Preparation *Attach one end of the thread to one corner of the handkerchief. Attach the other end to your table. Fold the handkerchief and place it on your table alongside the length of thread.*

● ● ● ● ● ● ● ● ● ● ● ● ● ● ●

1 Pick up the handkerchief and stand about 1m/3ft to the side of the table. Hold the handkerchief by the corner knotted to the thread. We will call this end A. The thread should pass under your right arm to the table

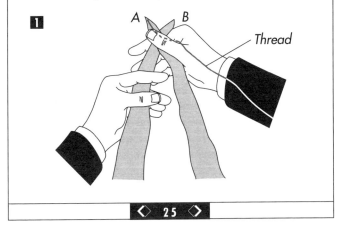

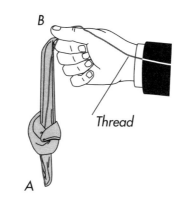

2

Thread

B

A

top. Do not worry about anybody seeing the thread. The attention of the audience is on you and what you do with the handkerchief.

2 What you do with the handkerchief is to take the diagonally opposite corner to end A in your left hand (we will call this end B). Twist the handkerchief into a rope by spinning it between your hands. You should not get caught up in the thread as you do this as it passes under your arm.

3 Bring end A across and over end B and hold both ends in your right hand, adjusting your right hand so the thread passes over your right thumb (illustration 1).

4 Reach through the loop with your left hand (moving your hand towards the audience), grasp end A with the thread and pull it back through the loop.

5 Pull your hands apart slowly so that a knot forms in the center (illustration 2). Unknown to the audience the thread passes through the loop in the knot. It is important the thread runs over your right thumb.

6 Release end A, so the handkerchief is held in the right hand. The thread is attached to the bottom corner A of the handkerchief and passes up through the knot, over your right thumb and across the table.

7 So if you move your right arm forward, the thread will pull end A up and through the knot (illustration 3). Gently move forward to pull end A up to your right hand. The knot will appear to melt away. When end A reaches your hand, release your hold of end B and grasp end A (illustration 4). Drop the handkerchief back on to your table, concluding your performance of the world's first untying knot!

3

B

A

Thread

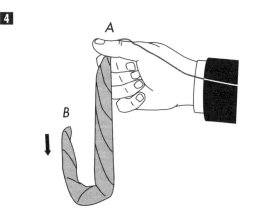

4

A

B

↓

This is a stunning visual effect that is in the repertoire of many of the world's best professional magicians. It is important that you spend plenty of time practicing, rehearsing and mastering this effect before you attempt to show it to anyone.

It is also possible to perform this effect without using a table. Instead of attaching the thread to the table you use a shorter length of thread, and attach one end to the handkerchief and the other end to a bead. The bead will dangle down to the floor. After you have tied the knot, put your right foot on the bead. The only other difference in the trick is that you move your right arm upwards instead of forwards to untie the knot.

   This method enables you to perform the effect almost impromptu.

PENETRATIONS

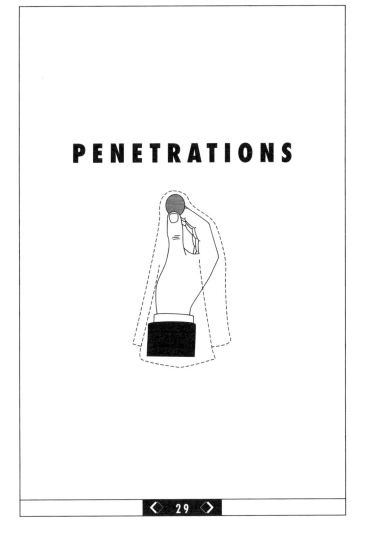

Effect *A silk handkerchief – representing the world famous escape artist Harry Houdini – escapes from a sealed glass tumbler.*

Requirements *Two different colored silk handkerchiefs, a large silk scarf, 25cm/10in of cotton thread, a glass tumbler and an elastic band.*

Preparation *Tie the cotton thread to one corner of the handkerchief that you want to "escape."*

●●●●●●●●●●●●●●●●●

1 Tell the audience about the exploits of the Great Houdini and his ability to escape from any confinement – prison cell, packing case, straitjacket or handcuffs. Explain that your audience are very fortunate because for the first time ever you are going to introduce the re-incarnation of Houdini – as a silk handkerchief!

1

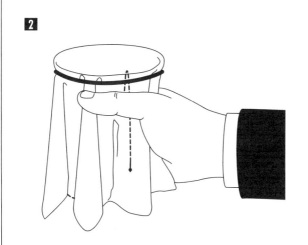

2 Display the "Houdini silk" to the audience and push it down into the bottom of the empty tumbler. As you do this make sure that you leave the thread hanging outside the glass.

3 Introduce the second handkerchief as a prison guard and stuff it into the tumbler on top of the first handkerchief (illustration 1).

4 To make extra sure that the handkerchief is unable to escape, throw the scarf over the mouth of the tumbler and hold it in place with the elastic band (illustration 2). You could call this the padded cell – or perhaps this is taking the analogy a bit too far!

5 Now tell the audience that this escape used to take 30 minutes! But today you intend to double that time! After a suitable build-up of tension, reach up under the scarf and take hold of the thread (this will be a lot easier if you tied a knot in the end of the thread).

6 Pull the thread, and the Houdini silk will be pulled out of the glass. You need to experiment to make sure that you are using an elastic band that is loose enough to enable you to do this.

7 Once the corner of the handkerchief has been pulled past the rubber band, grab hold of it and pull it sharply downwards, making it look as if the silk has penetrated through the bottom of the glass. Houdini lives on to escape once again!

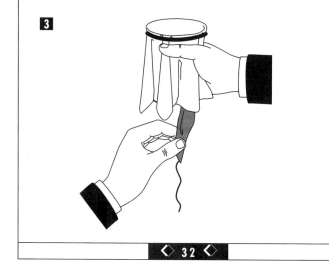

This is based on the "Dissolving Knot" and it is highly recommended that you learn and perfect that effect before attempting this one.

Effect *The magician displays two silk handkerchiefs, which are then twisted into ropes. A spectator holds one outstretched between his hands. The handkerchiefs are securely knotted around each other, creating two knotted linked loops of silk. Like the classic "Chinese Linking Rings" the handkerchiefs seem to melt apart with their knots still intact.*

1

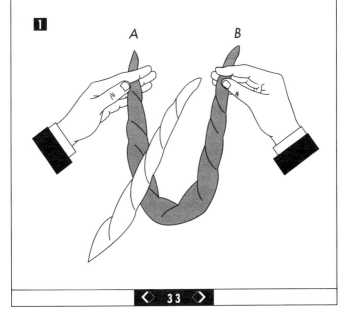

Requirements *Two silk handkerchiefs 45 x 45cm/18 x 18in, preferably of contrasting colors.*

Preparation *None.*

• • • • • • • • • • • • • • • •

1 Hold the first handkerchief by its diagonally opposite corners and twist it into a rope. Hand it to a member of the audience, requesting them to hold on tightly to the two ends.

2 Twist the second handkerchief and thread it underneath the first (illustration 1). Hold an end of your handkerchief in each hand.

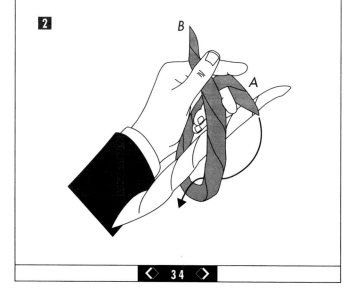

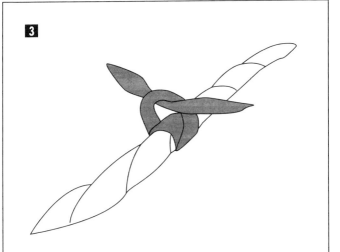

3 Move the righthand end (end B) over to the left hand and clip the two ends exactly as in the "Dissolving Knot" (illustration 2). Insert your right hand through the loop and grab end A. Pull this end back through the loop to form the "Dissolving Knot."

4 Pull the two ends of your rope in opposite directions to tighten to the knot. As you do this, keep your left second finger in the small loop. When the knot becomes tight you can slide out your left finger and the knot will hold itself together.

5 Loop your handkerchief underneath the spectator's handkerchief again and tie a regular secure reef knot (see Glossary) above the slip knot to make "an unbreakable circle of silk" (illustration 3).

6 Ask the spectator to tie the two ends of his handkerchief together in a secure knot. As they do this, hold on to the slip knot to ensure it is not accidentally pulled apart. It seems that the two handkerchiefs are now securely linked together.

7 Ask the spectator to hold on to the two ends of their handkerchief. You do the same with yours. Get the audience to blow on the handkerchiefs as you gently pull. The slip knot will dissolve and the two handkerchiefs will melt apart in a very magical fashion.

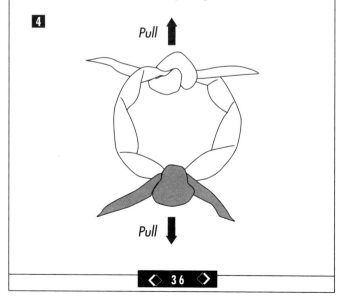

4

Pull

Pull

Effect *The magician sticks a pencil through the center of a borrowed handkerchief without damaging it!*

Requirements *The largest handkerchief you can borrow (a cloth table napkin will do), a pencil 8cm/3in long and a piece of newspaper 30 x 30cm/12 x 12in.*

Preparation *None.*

● ● ● ● ● ● ● ● ● ● ● ● ● ● ● ●

1 Invite two spectators to assist you. Have them each hold on to two corners of the borrowed handkerchief and stretch it between them so that it is parallel with the floor.

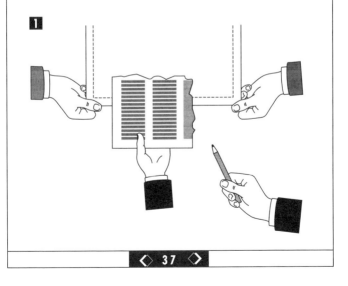

2

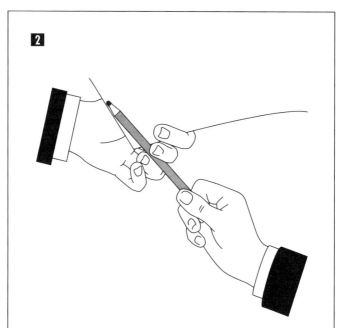

2 Hold the pencil in the right hand with the point downwards. Hold the square of newspaper in the left hand over the center of the handkerchief.

3 The right hand moves the pencil under the center of the handkerchief and pushes upwards. When the pencil fails to penetrate, relax and bring the right hand out from underneath. The left hand moves to the edge of the handkerchief.

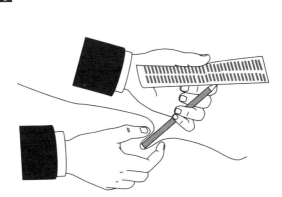

4 Look at the pencil and say, "Of course, the pencil should be pointed end up." Turn the pencil around.

5 As the right hand moves back under the handkerchief you perform the all-important secret move. The left second and third fingers clip the pencil (illustration 2). This action is covered by the newspaper.

6 The right hand does not pause, but continues to move underneath to the center of the handkerchief as though it still contained the pencil.

7 The left hand moves forward on top of the handkerchief back to the center.

8 Through the fabric the right hand grips the blunt end of the pencil. With the left hand, push the newspaper down over the pencil (illustration 3). The pencil tears a hole in the newspaper as though it has just been pushed through the handkerchief.

9 Pull the pencil all the way through the hole in the newspaper (illustration 4). After sufficient build-up and suspense – "You'll be the only person with air conditioning in their handkerchief!" – remove the newspaper to show the handkerchief is completely unharmed!

10 Thank your two volunteers (and the handkerchief!) as they all return to the safety of the audience!

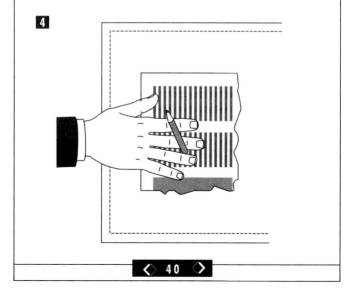

Effect *A coin and a handkerchief are both borrowed from members of the audience. The coin visibly passes through the center of the handkerchief, leaving it undamaged!*

Requirements *A coin and a handkerchief (both can be borrowed).*

Preparation *None.*

● ● ● ● ● ● ● ● ● ● ● ● ● ● ● ●

1 Display the coin at the tips of the right thumb and first two fingers so that the audience see one side of the coin. Your left hand drapes the handkerchief over the coin and right hand so that the coin is under the approximate center of the handkerchief (illustration 1).

1

2 As the left hand is adjusting the handkerchief over the coin, your left thumb secretly lifts a bit of cloth behind the coin and folds it behind the right thumb. When you remove your left hand you will have two layers of cloth clipped between your right thumb and the back of the coin (illustration 2), preparing you for the secret move.

3 With your left hand grab the front edge of the handkerchief and lift it back and over the coin. This displays the coin still in position under the center of the handkerchief. When you cover the coin again your left

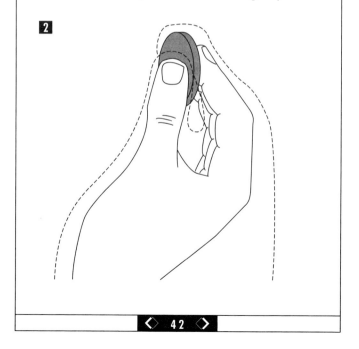

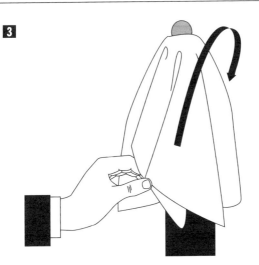

3

hand takes both edges of the handkerchief over the coin (illustration 3). Now your right thumb is holding the coin outside the handkerchief. The clipped piece of cloth prevents the handkerchief falling away after you have done this (illustration 4).

4 With your left hand, grip the coin from above through the layers of the handkerchief. Your right hand now lets go of the coin and twists the lower part of the handkerchief to reveal the shape of the coin (illustration 5).

5 Slowly push the coin upwards with your right hand, as your left hand takes the edge of the coin – as it magically penetrates through the handkerchief.

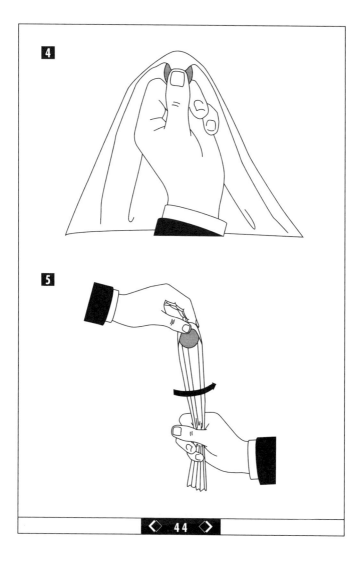

◇ SHRINKING COIN ◇

Effect A coin, a handkerchief and a finger ring are all borrowed from members of the audience. The coin is wrapped in the center of the handkerchief, and the ring threaded over all four corners to trap it inside. Despite this secure set-up the coin manages to pass through the ring and escape from inside the handkerchief – much to the audience's amazement!

Requirements A handkerchief, a large coin and a finger ring – the effect is much more impressive if all these items are borrowed from members of the audience, but it is worth having your own standing by ready to use if necessary. If you do have to use your own props, have them examined by the audience before you begin the effect.

Preparation There is no specific preparation for this effect, but it is highly recommended that you master the "Coin Through Handkerchief" effect before attempting to perform this one.

●●●●●●●●●●●●●●●●●

1

1 Have the handkerchief, coin and finger ring examined by the audience. Then collect them together and invite two members of the audience up to assist you.

2 Display the coin and wrap it in the handkerchief as described in the "Coin Through Handkerchief" effect so that the coin is held outside the handkerchief (illustration 1). Twist the lower part of the handkerchief to reveal the shape of the apparently trapped coin (but do not perform the penetration).

3 Hold the coin through the handkerchief in the left hand so that the coin is resting flat against the left fingers. The "open" side (which would reveal the coin) is resting against the fingertips.

4 Have a spectator thread the finger ring over all four corners of the handkerchief. As they do this hold the coin tightly with the left hand, and with the right hand hold the handkerchief just above the coin to prevent it unwrapping.

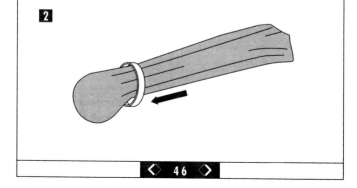

2

5 Have the spectator slide the ring down the handkerchief until it reaches the coin (illustration 2). The ring will lock the coin in position and prevent the handkerchief unwrapping. You can now ask two spectators to each hold two corners of the handkerchief so that it is parallel with the floor (illustration 3) while you let go of the coin. The coin and ring are both below the handkerchief.

6 Point out the situation to the audience – the coin is trapped in the center of the handkerchief by the ring. It cannot escape as the hole in the middle of the ring is much smaller than the coin.

7 Reach under the handkerchief with both hands. With your left hand slide the ring up the handkerchief to give you sufficient slack to release the coin into your right hand (illustration 4). Until the end of the trick your left hand remains under the handkerchief holding on to the ring and the center of the handkerchief, so that your spectators believe the coin is still trapped inside.

8 Conceal the coin in your right hand in the finger palm position. To finger palm a coin, simply clip it at the base of the fingers by slightly closing your hand until the coin is held securely in position. (When you hold your hands naturally they are usually slightly closed.) The audience believe the coin is trapped in the handkerchief and they have no reason to suspect it is anywhere else. If you do not draw attention to your right hand, your audience won't bother about it either.

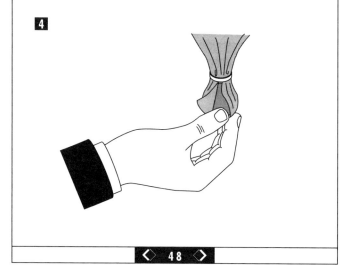

9 Bring your apparently empty right hand over the top of the handkerchief to the middle over the "well" in the center. Your right hand secretly releases the finger-palmed coin into this well in the handkerchief. Under the handkerchief the left fingers catch the coin and grip it through the fabric.

10 Wave your right hand over the center in a mystical fashion as though you are performing a "magical pass" over the well. This was your reason for moving your hand to the center of the handkerchief.

11 Ask the spectators to slowly pull on their corners of the handkerchief. Very slowly with your left hand release the coin. It will appear to rise up out of the center of the handkerchief as though it is passing through the center of the ring. This is a very magical moment when done slowly and should get a great round of applause from your audience – and a gasp of amazement from your two "hanky holders."

12 Allow your two assistants to continue pulling on their corners until the handkerchief is stretched flat between them with the coin lying on top in the center. Bring your left hand out from underneath the handkerchief with the borrowed finger ring to show that it is undamaged. You point out that the impossible must have occurred. The only explanation can be that the coin "shrank" to pass through the ring and then grew back to its original size. You can finish by saying, "I've heard of deflating currency but this is ridiculous!"

COLOR CHANGES

Effect *The magician displays a handkerchief. As the magician's hand is passed over it the handkerchief changes color.*

Requirements *Two different colored silk handkerchiefs, a metal ring with diameter 2.5cm/1in and sewing equipment.*

Preparation *Place one handkerchief on top of the other and sew them together just above the center with a line of stitching about 5cm/2in long. Sew the top corner of the rear handkerchief to the far side of the metal ring. Poke the top corner A of the upper handkerchief through the ring (illustration 1). Fold up the lower corner B of the upper handkerchief and sew it to the near side of the metal ring (illustration 2). Fold the set-up in half lengthwise so that the lower handkerchief covers the folded top handkerchief (illustration 3). Sew the two sides of the outer handkerchief together, ensuring that the inner silk does not bulge out too much, but lies flat.*

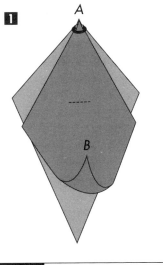

Grasp the tip A of the inner silk through the ring and pull the ring down. This will transpose the handkerchiefs, exposing the inner silk and concealing the outer one. Sew up the sides of the now outer handkerchief to prevent the inner silk from being seen.

• • • • • • • • • • • • • • • •

1 Display the handkerchief to your audience.

2 With the left hand grasp the tip of the handkerchief sticking out of the ring.

3 Pull the ring down over the silk with the right hand. To the audience it appears that the handkerchief changes color as your hand passes over it (illustration 4). As the handkerchief changes color, shake it slightly.

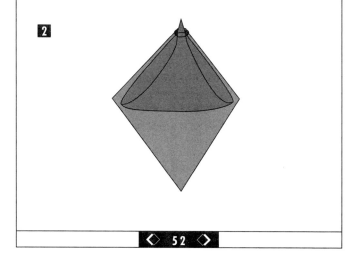

4 You can end the effect there or turn the handkerchief upside down and repeat the process to restore the handkerchief to its original color.

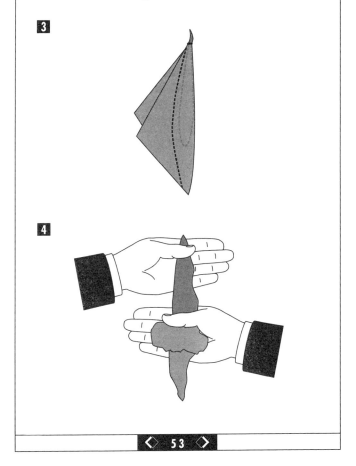

Effect *A red silk handkerchief with white borders is pulled through the hand and changes to a green silk handkerchief with white borders.*

Requirements *A white handkerchief, plus two slightly smaller ones, one red and the other green.*

Preparation *Make a special handkerchief by sewing the two colored handkerchiefs on each side of the white one (illustration 1).*

● ● ● ● ● ● ● ● ● ● ● ● ● ● ●

1

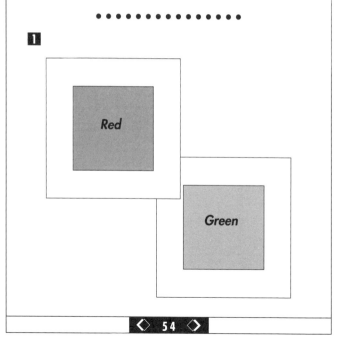

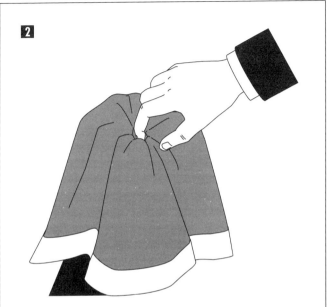

1 Pick up the handkerchief, displaying the red side, and spread it out over your open left hand.

2 Form your left hand into a fist under the cover of the handkerchief.

3 With the right forefinger push the center of the handkerchief into the left fist (illustration 2).

4 With your right hand reach underneath and grab the center of the handkerchief. Pull it down through your fist and into view (illustration 3).

5 The handkerchief is now green. Show the green side to the audience, making sure that you keep the red side hidden.

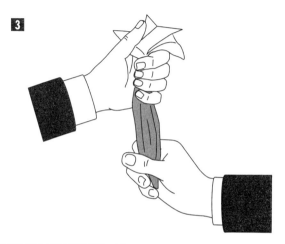

TONY SLYDINI (1901-1991)

Slydini is generally regarded as one of the fathers of modern close-up magic. Like Dai Vernon, he was an inspiration for many magicians to master sleight of hand. He moved to the East coast of America from Italy in his youth and went on to have his own studio in New York for private performances and teaching. Handkerchief magic like the "Dissolving Knot" and "Over the Head" became "real" in his hands.

Effect *After the wave of a magic wand the magician produces a silk handkerchief from his hands, which were empty moments before. Another wave of the wand and the handkerchief changes color!*

Requirements *A magic wand and two contrasting silk handkerchiefs – say, red and yellow.*

Preparation *Fold the four corners of each handkerchief to the center. Then roll each one into a tube and wrap them alongside each other around one end of the wand (illustration 1). To perform this as an opener, hold the wand in your right hand, with your hand concealing the handkerchiefs. To perform later, set the wand on your table with other props covering the handkerchiefs.*

• • • • • • • • • • • • • • • •

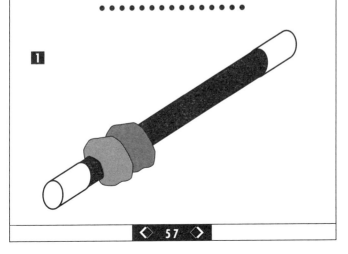

1

2

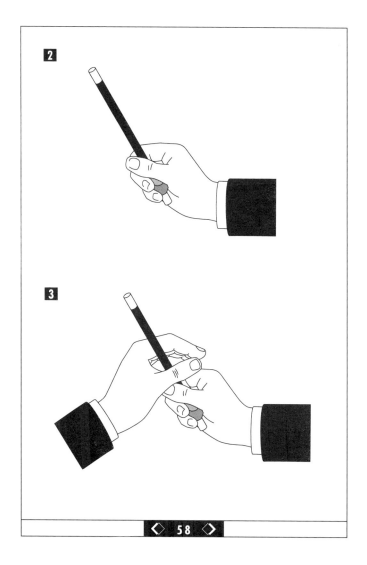

3

1 Begin with the wand in the right hand (illustration 2). Tap the empty left hand with the free end of the wand as you say, "My left hand is empty . . ."

2 Slide the left hand up the wand until the two hands meet (illustration 3). The left hand grasps the end of the wand, covering the two handkerchiefs. The wand pivots to the right and the right hand is shown to be empty as you say, ". . . and the right too."

3 The left hand keeps hold of the lower of the two handkerchiefs, as the right hand takes the wand back concealing the other handkerchief on the wand. We will assume the handkerchief in the left hand is red and the one still on the wand is yellow.

4

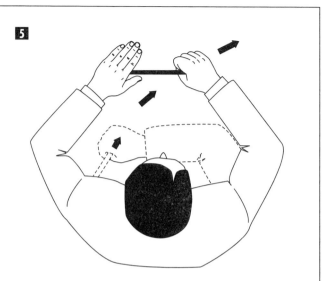

5

4 The right hand places the wand under the left arm so that the handkerchief is concealed under the left armpit and the free end sticks out in front (illustration 4).

5 The right hand points to the left hand, which reaches forward and snaps out the red silk handkerchief – apparently from nowhere!

6 When the applause from this production has died down, continue by rolling up the red handkerchief into a ball. This goes into your left hand while you make a magical pass with your right hand. Open your left hand to show that nothing has happened.

7 Roll the handkerchief up again, but this time keep it concealed in your right hand while pretending it is your closed left fist.

8 The right hand (holding the red handkerchief concealed) reaches for the free end of the wand and moves it down (illustration 5) behind your left arm (which acts as a screen) and into the left hand which opens briefly to secretly "steal" the yellow handkerchief from the end of the wand. The wand continues moving.

9 Wave the wand over the closed left fist and open it to show that the handkerchief has now changed color.

When performed correctly this is a very baffling and convincing effect, but it is highly recommended that you rehearse it many times in front of a mirror to ensure that your timing is correct and that in step 8 the yellow handkerchief remains concealed from the audience.

HOUDIN AND HOUDINI

In 1856 Robert Houdin was sent by the French government to Algiers to quell the revolution by proving that French magic was stronger than African magic! On his return he wrote of his adventures in The Memoirs of Robert Houdin. *Nearly 30 years later a young Hungarian boy in America read the book and decided to become a magician. He based his stage name on that of his hero – and became Houdini!*

PRODUCTIONS

Effect *After showing that two tubes are both completely empty, the magician produces silk handkerchiefs and ribbons from inside.*

Requirements *Two tubes about 30cm/12in high and 15cm/6in diameter, which fit one inside the other (it may be easiest to make the tubes to size using stiff paper held together with paper clips), a paper clip, about 15cm/6in of dark thread, elastic bands and your production "load" – ribbons and silk handkerchiefs.*

1

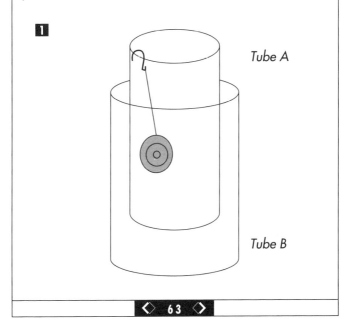

Tube A

Tube B

Preparation *Roll up the handkerchiefs and ribbons into a compact bundle and hold it together with the elastic bands. Bend the paper clip into an S-shaped hook. Attach one end of the thread to the hook and the other end to one of the elastic bands. Hook the clip over the top edge of the thinner tube (tube A) with the bundle dangling inside out of sight. We will call the wider of the two tubes tube B.*

Set tubes A and B next to each other on the table.

● ● ● ● ● ● ● ● ● ● ● ● ● ● ● ● ●

2

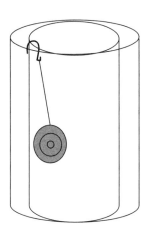

1 Pick up both tubes, one in each hand. Hold up tube B so that the audience can see through it and see that it is empty.

2 Slide tube A into the top of tube B, making sure that the hook clips on to the top of tube B (illustration 2).

3 Allow tube A to slide out of the bottom of tube B. The bundle should remain hanging out of sight inside tube B. You can now hold up tube A to show the audience that it is completely empty.

4 Slide tube A back into tube B from the bottom, so that the bundle is now hanging inside both tubes (illustration 3). Roll up your sleeves and show the audience that your hands are completely empty. Reach inside the tubes and remove the elastic bands from around the

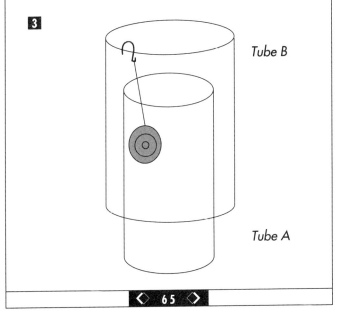

Tube B

Tube A

bundle. Dramatically remove the ribbons and handkerchiefs from inside the nested tubes (illustration 4).

4

THE ZOMBIE BALL

This effect is one of the true classics of magic. A silver ball floats underneath a silk handkerchief without any visible means of support. At times it comes to balance at the top edge of the handkerchief before continuing its mysterious movements. This effect is a great piece of situation comedy when performed by Ali Bongo, the "Shriek" of Araby.

◇ APPEARING SILK HANKY ◇

Effect *This is a startling opening effect. The magician shows both hands empty. After making a grab in the air a silk handkerchief appears in the magician's hands!*

Requirements *A silk handkerchief about 45 x 45cm/18 x 18in.*

Preparation *Spread the handkerchief out flat on a table. Fold the four corners into the middle so that they almost touch (illustrations 1 and 2). Repeat, folding the four new corners into the center. Continue folding until you have a bundle about 5cm/2in across.*

1　　　　　　　**2**

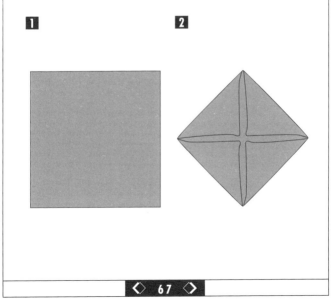

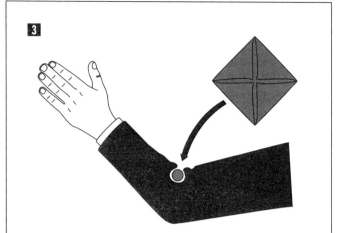

Place the folded handkerchief in the bend of your elbow (illustration 3) just before you begin your performance. If you keep your arm bent the handkerchief will remain concealed.

• • • • • • • • • • • • • • •

This effect is over in just a few seconds, but it appears to be quite magical.

1 Show the audience that both your hands are empty by wiggling your fingers.

2 Look upwards. Quickly reach up with both hands and, as you do this, straighten your arms. The handkerchief will be propelled into the air (illustration 4).

3 Catch the handkerchief between your hands. It seems to have appeared in mid-air.

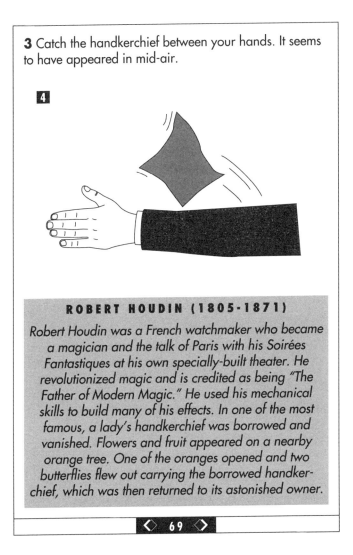

ROBERT HOUDIN (1805-1871)

Robert Houdin was a French watchmaker who became a magician and the talk of Paris with his Soirées Fantastiques at his own specially-built theater. He revolutionized magic and is credited as being "The Father of Modern Magic." He used his mechanical skills to build many of his effects. In one of the most famous, a lady's handkerchief was borrowed and vanished. Flowers and fruit appeared on a nearby orange tree. One of the oranges opened and two butterflies flew out carrying the borrowed handkerchief, which was then returned to its astonished owner.

Effect *The magician displays an arrow with a mind of its own – and then produces a handkerchief from inside.*

Requirements *A square sheet of thick paper, extra paper, invisible sellotape and a silk handkerchief.*

Preparation *Fold the piece of paper into quarters lengthwise. Stick an extra piece of paper on to one panel to make a secret pocket with a flap. Then make the paper into a tube by sticking two edges together with sellotape (illustrations 1 and 2). Hide the handkerchief inside the pocket. Flatten the tube down and cut it as shown in illustration 3 to make a nose and a tail.*

• • • • • • • • • • • • • • • •

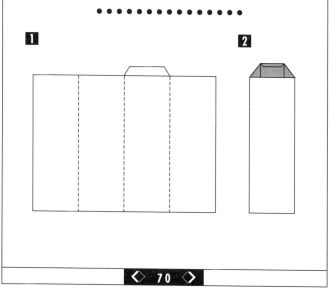

1

2

3

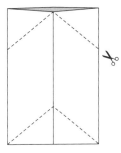

1 Show the arrow pointing to your left and tell your audience that they must never trust arrows as they might be pointing the wrong way.

2 Turn the arrow around so that it is pointing to the right. Say, "See, it is easy to move an arrow. Sometimes it changes direction so quickly it seems like magic!"

3 As you say this you squeeze the two outer edges together so that the tube opens out and folds flat the other way. The arrow is now pointing left again.

4 You can turn the arrow left and right by repeating step 3 as many times as you wish.

5 Finally conclude by saying, "Of course, you can't trust me – I'm a magician. I was just trying to pull the wool over your eyes!" As you say this, reach into the end of the arrow and pull the silk handkerchief out of the secret pocket (illustration 5).

4

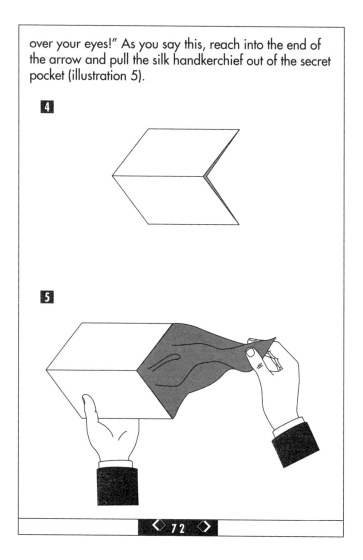

5

◇ EGGS FROM NOWHERE ◇

Effect The magician shows the audience an ordinary handkerchief. He folds it in half and an egg rolls out from inside. He tips the egg into a basket. Another egg appears . . . and another . . . and another. This apparently unlimited number of eggs are shaken, one at a time, from the handkerchief into the basket. The magician sets the handkerchief down to one side, reaches into the basket, removes one egg and breaks it into a glass to prove it is real. Walking forward with the basket the magician throws the contents at the audience! To the audience's surprise – and relief – the eggs have been transformed into a basketful of confetti!

Requirements An opaque handkerchief 60 x 60cm/24 x 24in, a small basket, a plastic egg, a real egg, a glass, some thread to match the color of the handkerchief and a supply of confetti.

Preparation Attach the plastic egg to one end of a piece of thread about 30cm/12in long. Attach the other end of the thread to the center of one edge of the handkerchief, so that the egg hangs just below the center of the handkerchief when the handkerchief is held up (illustration 2). Fill the basket with confetti and hide the real egg inside. Fold the handkerchief and place it next to the basket with the false egg resting on the confetti inside the basket next to the real egg (illustration 1).

• • • • • • • • • • • • • •

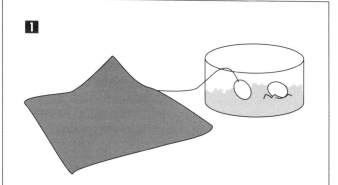

1 Lift up the handkerchief by the edge which does not have the thread attached. The egg will remain hidden in the basket while you show both sides of the handkerchief to the audience. Say, "As you can see, there are no chickens hidden in my handkerchief!" The audience will wonder what you are talking about. They will soon find out . . .

2 Lay the threaded hem of the handkerchief over the top of the basket so that it covers the plastic egg. Show that your hands are empty and roll up your sleeves, saying, "No chickens up my sleeves!"

TOP TIPS FOR TRICKSTERS

Magic with silk handkerchiefs is ideally suited for female magicians because the props involved have a definite "feminine" feel to them.

3 Pick up the handkerchief by the corners of the threaded hem and pull the hem tight between your hands. Lift the handkerchief straight up away from the basket and table. The thread will pull the egg out of the basket and it will dangle concealed behind the handkerchief (illustration 2).

4 Bring the top two corners together in your left hand (illustration 3), concealing the egg in the folds of the handkerchief. Your right hand holds the two lower corners together and moves up to the right until the folded handkerchief is held horizontally.

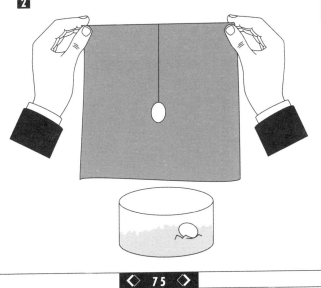

5 Move the handkerchief so that it is to your right of the basket. Lift your right hand slightly and shake the egg out of the handkerchief (illustration 4) so that it falls into the basket and lands on the confetti. Now the audience will understand all this talk of invisible chickens!

6 Rest the handkerchief back on top of the basket. The corners in the right hand go on the table in front of the basket. The right hand moves up to the left hand to take hold of one of the two corners being held in the left hand.

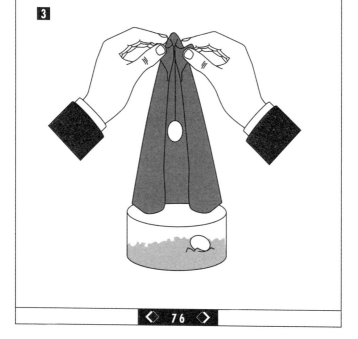

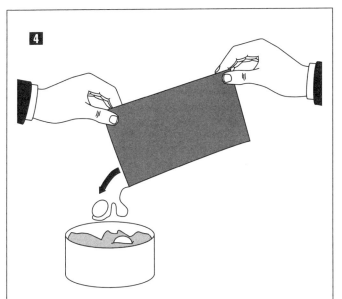

7 Draw your hands apart and raise the top two corners, again secretly lifting the egg out of the basket behind the handkerchief.

8 Repeat steps 4 and 5 to produce a second egg – really it is the second showing of the same one!

TOP TIPS FOR TRICKSTERS

When entertaining children with effects with different colored handkerchiefs it is a good "bit of business" to get your colors wrong and allow them to correct you.

9 Repeat steps 4 to 7 as many times as you wish to give the impression of an apparently endless supply of magical eggs.

10 To conclude, lift the handkerchief and egg out of the basket for the last time (step 7) and set the handkerchief down on the table, ensuring that the egg is hidden inside the folds of the handkerchief.

11 Remove the real egg from the basket and break it into the glass to prove it is the real thing!

12 Finally pick up the basket and walk towards the audience. They believe it is full of real eggs, so make sure they can't see inside the basket. Throw the contents towards the audience. They will be surprised – and relieved – to be showered with confetti. This makes a good finale to a show!

HARRY BLACKSTONE (1885-1965)

Harry Blackstone toured the theaters of America in the mid 1900s with his spectacular illusion show. One of the highlights of his show was his "Haunted Hanky" effect, in which a borrowed handkerchief apparently became possessed by spirits and began moving and dancing around the stage! This effect is still performed today by his son, Harry Blackstone Jr., who travels the world with his own illusion show keeping the name Blackstone up in lights.

ADVANCED
HANDKERCHIEF
TRICKS

SPECTACULAR VANISHES

Effect *The magician places a coin under a handkerchief. One by one a number of spectators place their hands under the handkerchief to make sure the coin is still there. Despite this tight security the coin vanishes. Even though the audience can all examine the handkerchief and the magician, they cannot find the coin.*

Requirements *A handkerchief and a coin. Both can be borrowed from members of the audience.*

Preparation *You need one other vital thing, and that is a secret helper! Before your performance get a member of the audience on your side and tell them to take the coin when they feel under the handkerchief and keep it concealed in their hand!*

● ● ● ● ● ● ● ● ● ● ● ● ● ● ● ●

1

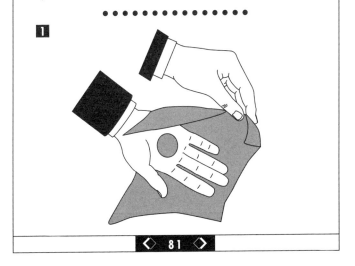

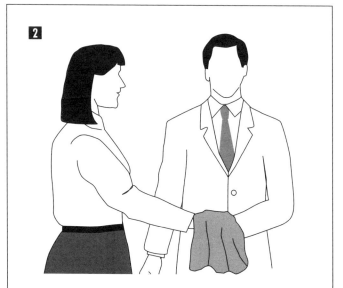

1 Borrow a handkerchief and a coin from members of the audience. Explain that the audience are going to act as your jury for this performance.

2 Roll up your sleeves so the audience cannot suspect that the coin goes up one of your sleeves.

TOP TIPS FOR TRICKSTERS

To prevent your silk handkerchiefs from becoming frayed at the edges you can double hem them. Fold over the original hem and sew them again.

3 Put the coin on the palm of your hand and cover it with the handkerchief (illustration 1).

4 Invite spectators up to feel under the handkerchief to check that the coin is definitely there and that you haven't sneaked it out by sleight of hand.

5 Make sure that your secret helper is the last one to feel under the handkerchief (illustration 2). You hand them the coin which they keep concealed in their hand!

6 You can now remove the handkerchief and show that the coin has vanished.

7 Meet up with your secret helper after the show to split the profits!

It makes the effect more convincing if your secret helper behaves like a very cynical critic who really does not believe that it can be done. Then nobody will suspect that they actually did the trick for you!

CARL HERTZ

Carl Hertz was an American magician who moved to Britain. In the UK he became well-known on the music halls – particularly for one trick which had everybody talking. He vanished a metal birdcage with a live bird inside from the tips of his fingers. Many suspected that the bird was harmed and so Hertz was called to perform it at the House of Commons!

Effect *The magician places a silk handkerchief in a brown paper bag. When the bag is torn open the handkerchief has vanished!*

Requirements *Two brown grocery bags, scissors, glue and the handkerchief to be vanished.*

Preparation *Cut out a portion of the front panel from one bag. Glue it along three sides as in illustration 1. Then stick it inside the duplicate bag to make a secret pocket (illustration 2). Fold the bag flat on your table.*

• • • • • • • • • • • • • • • •

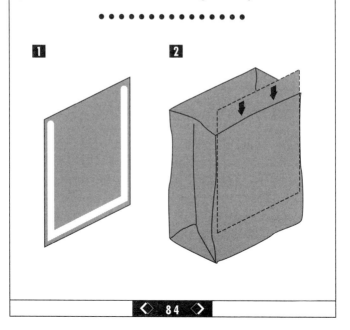

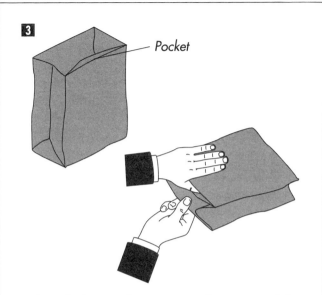

3

Pocket

1 Pick up the bag, at the same time slipping your left thumb into the secret pocket. Open up the bag, keeping your thumb in position inside the bag (illustration 3).

2 Place the handkerchief inside the bag. Really you place it in the secret pocket.

3 Move your left thumb outside the secret pocket to hold it closed (illustration 4).

4 Holding the bag with your left hand, tear it open with your right hand – to show that the bag is empty and the handkerchief has vanished (illustration 5).

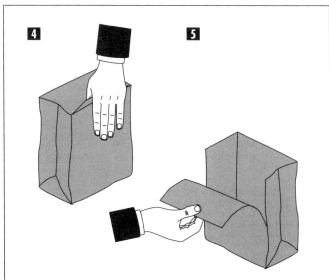

You can use the paper bag for many other effects. For example, by having another handkerchief hidden in the bottom of the bag, you can apparently make knots appear on the handkerchief – or make it change color completely. Or you can put several handkerchiefs in the bag and apparently make them join together in a chain or loop.

You could perform a version of "Twentieth Century Silks" without the fake handkerchief, by putting a duplicate set (with the multi-colored silk tied between the other two) in the bottom of the bag. You can probably think up many other effects using this vanish.

MENTAL MAGIC

Effect *The magician explains that there are three handkerchiefs – red, white and blue – tied together in a certain order inside a container. The container is in full view of the audience. A member of the audience is invited to assist. They tie three duplicate handkerchiefs – red, white and blue – in a chain in any order that they choose. The magician then reaches into the container and pulls out the three hidden handkerchiefs tied in exactly the same order!*

Requirements *A container, six handkerchiefs – two red, two blue and two white – and three small rubber bands.*

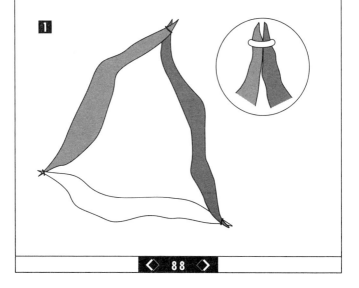

Preparation *Arrange one set of red, white and blue handkerchiefs in a loop by fastening the ends together with the rubber bands (illustration 1). Put the handkerchiefs in the container, and place the container on a table in full view of the audience. Ensure that the audience cannot see into the container.*

● ● ● ● ● ● ● ● ● ● ● ● ● ● ● ●

1 Explain that there are three handkerchiefs tied together in the container. If you wish, you can tip the container forward slightly so that the audience can see the handkerchiefs resting inside.

2 Invite a member of the audience to assist you – preferably somebody you have never met before, to dispel any suspicion of collusion.

3 Hand the spectator the duplicate set of three handkerchiefs and ask them to tie them together in any order they wish.

4 Note the colors of the handkerchiefs at each end of the chain. Reach into the container and separate those colors. For example, if the spectator's chain is white-blue-red, reach into the container and separate the white and red handkerchiefs. Then lift the handkerchiefs out of the box and show that the order matches that chosen by the spectator exactly!

5 Show that the container is empty, proving that there were only three handkerchiefs inside.

Effect *The magician displays a sealed prediction. A number of different colored squares are dropped into the middle of a handkerchief and a member of the audience reaches in and removes one square. The prediction reveals that the magician knew which color would be chosen. Spooky!*

Requirements *Two identical patterned pocket handkerchiefs, several small squares of card (about 2.5cm/1in square) all different colors (red, yellow, blue, green, orange, brown, black and white) and several squares of card all the same color (red) and a prediction reading "You will choose red."*

1

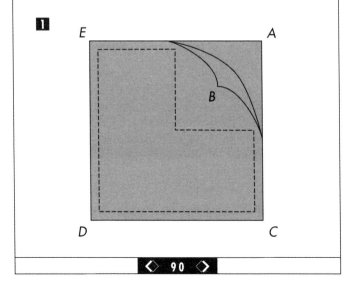

Preparation *You have to ensure that your volunteer chooses a red card by "forcing" it on them. To do this, you need to make a special handkerchief with a secret pocket. Place the two handkerchiefs one on top of the other and sew them together as shown in illustration 1 to make a secret pocket in one corner. In this secret pocket you put all the identical colored (red) squares. You need to set up the handkerchief so that you can leave it on your table, and pick it up without any of the hidden squares spilling out.*

● ● ● ● ● ● ● ● ● ● ● ● ● ● ●

1 Hand your sealed prediction to a member of the audience, who will be the "guardian of the envelope."

2 Hold the handkerchief in one hand by the secret pocket corner. Fold up the other three corners to make a bag. After showing all the colored squares to be different, drop them into the center of the handkerchief (illustration 2). Make sure they do not go into the secret pocket or you'll be in real trouble!

3 Shake up the handkerchief to mix the squares and ask a spectator to dip into the handkerchief and take out one square – this will be their freely chosen color. When you offer the handkerchief to the spectator you actually open up one side of the secret pocket, so that they reach into the compartment full of red squares. Unknown to them, it doesn't matter which square they pull out – it's going to be red!

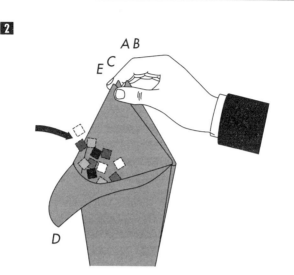

4 After the spectator has shown everyone their selected red square, dump the handkerchief to one side. Do not open the handkerchief again, as someone may see that the one red square is still among the selection of different colors! And be particularly careful not to let all the red squares fall out, or you will look very stupid!

5 Ask the "guardian of the envelope" to open it and read out your prediction. Once again the wonder magician has successfully predicted the future!

You can use the fake handkerchief to perform many other similar effects.

IMPOSSIBLE PENETRATIONS

This is apparently extraordinary and impossible penetration effect works on the fiendishly simple principle of secretly turning the glass upside down under the cover of the handkerchief.

Effect *A handkerchief is placed inside a drinking glass. It is then trapped inside it by placing a second handkerchief over the mouth of the glass, and securing it with a tight rubber band. Even though a member of the audience holds on to the glass, the handkerchief still manages to escape!*

Requirements *Two cotton handkerchiefs, a rubber band and a straight-sided drinking glass (that is, the diameter of the base and the mouth should be the same).*

Preparation *None.*

● ● ● ● ● ● ● ● ● ● ● ● ● ● ●

1

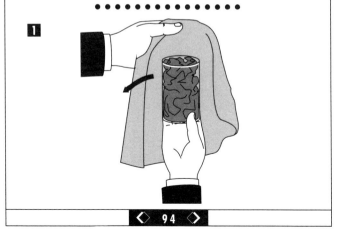

2

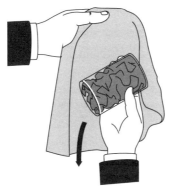

1 Ask a member of the audience to examine the glass to ensure there are no trap doors, secret passages or hidden keys to enable the handkerchief to escape! Meanwhile the handkerchief that is to escape can be subjected to an extensive "body search."

2 When the props have been examined, take them back and hold the empty drinking glass with the tips of the fingers and thumb of your right hand. Ask a member of the audience to put the handkerchief in the glass, and push it down to the bottom. It is important that you use a large handkerchief, so that when the glass is turned upside down it will not fall out, but cling to the glass.

3 To make an "air-tight container" you apparently drape the second handkerchief over the mouth of the glass and seal it with the elastic band. But in fact it is here that you perform the secret move! Bring the

3

handkerchief up in front of the glass to cover it from the audience's view for just a moment. At this moment your right hand relaxes its grip on the bottom of the glass and pivots it between your thumb and fingers, turning the glass upside down.

4 The left hand drapes its handkerchief over the now reversed glass and the right hand. Grip the glass with the left hand through the handkerchief and remove the right hand from under the handkerchief. Pick up the elastic band and apparently seal the top of the glass. In reality you are sealing the bottom!

5 Ask a member of the audience to come up and hold on to the sides of the glass. Ensure they do not put their fingers too near the elastic band, or they may feel that the "top" has sealed over with glass and realize it is really the bottom of the glass!

6 Show that both your hands are empty, roll up your sleeves and then dramatically reach under the covering handkerchief and pull out the handkerchief from inside the glass (illustration 3). Apparently it has penetrated right through the bottom of the glass.

7 After the applause has died down, take back the glass from the spectator. Reach underneath with the right hand and rest the edge of the mouth of the glass on the tips of the right thumb and fingers. With the left hand pull up the handkerchief so that the elastic band slides up too. When the elastic band has been released, pause while you pivot the glass in your right hand back to its starting position (illustration 4).

8 When the glass is back in its original position, take away the covering handkerchief. Show the empty undamaged glass and hand everything out for examination. Sit back and await more applause!

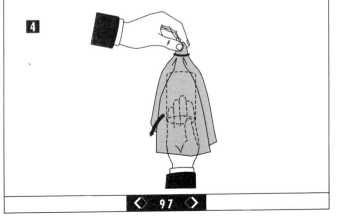

Effect *A silk handkerchief mysteriously passes through the center of a length of rope.*

Requirements *A silk handkerchief and a length of rope about 180cm/6ft long.*

Preparation *None.*

• • • • • • • • • • • • • • • •

1 Ask a spectator to hold the rope vertically with one end in each hand. Hold the handkerchief by diagonally opposite corners behind the spectator's rope and twist it into a silk "rope." Hold the left end A of the silk rope between the first and second fingers of the left hand.

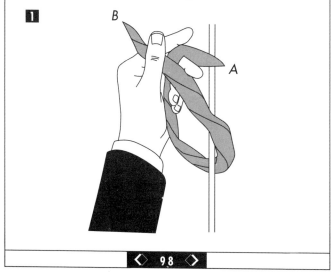

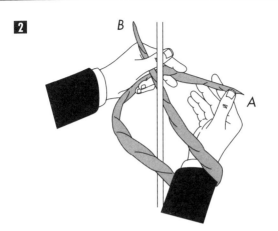

2 Bring the right end B of the silk rope in front of the spectator's rope and clip the end with the left thumb. Grip part of the right end B of the silk rope between the second and third fingers of the left hand (illustration 1). Clip part of end A with the left third and fourth fingers (illustration 2) and clip end B with the second finger.

3 Now put the right hand through the loop and pull end A of the silk back through the loop (illustration 2). Retain the grip of the left third and fourth fingers, and clip end B with the second finger to form a loop (illustration 3). Pull on end A to tighten the knot.

4 It looks as if the handkerchief is tied with a genuine knot, but it is really a slip knot. Bring end B around the front of the rope, to the back, and to the right again.

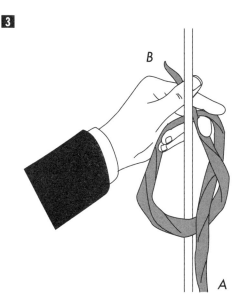

5 Tie the silk in a single knot in front of the rope, making sure that end A comes back to the right side when the knot is tied (illustrations 4 and 5).

6 Tell the spectator to hold the rope tightly. Pause to build up the tension and ensure that you have the attention of the audience. Grasp the silk near the knot and pull forward. The silk will come free and it looks as if it has passed right through the rope. The silk, the rope and the magician can all be examined!

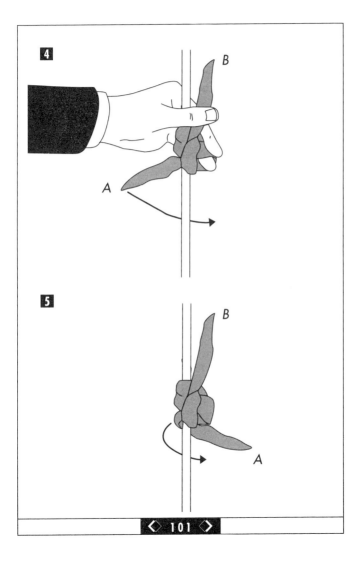

Effect *A silk handkerchief penetrates through the arm of a member of your audience.*

Requirements *A large silk handkerchief.*

Preparation *None.*

● ● ● ● ● ● ● ● ● ● ● ● ● ● ● ● ●

1 A lot of fun can be had in finding a victim – sorry volunteer – for you to try out your new experiment in painless surgery! When you find a willing spectator – or someone your audience would like you to use – invite them to stand alongside you.

2 This effect can be performed to make the handkerchief pass through a spectator's arm, leg or neck. The

1

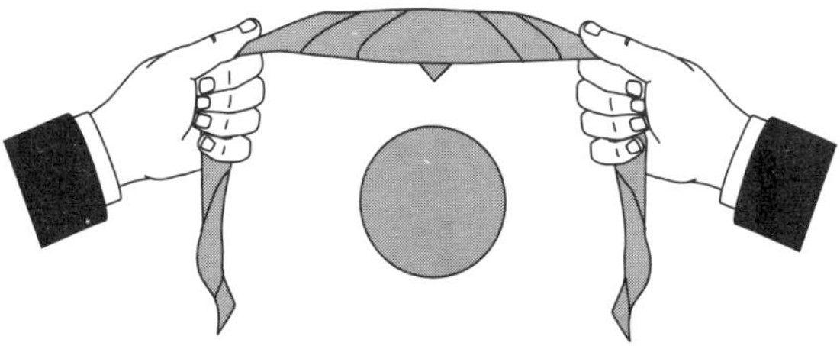

decision is yours, but will of course depend on the size of your handkerchief and the spectator involved! It will be described as though you are performing it with an arm!

3 Hold two diagonally opposite corners and twist the handkerchief into a rope (illustration 1). Explain that you are going to use the "cheese-wire method" to pull the handkerchief through the arm. It will look just like wire cutting through soft cheese!

4 Place the "rope" on top of the spectator's arm. Bring the ends below the arm and pretend to tie a knot (illustration 2). In fact you actually fold each end of the handkerchief back to make two loops behind the arm, and then twist these two loops together (illustration 3).

5 Pull the ends tight to keep the twisted loops in place. Bring the two ends back to the front, being careful not cross them over behind the arm. Tie the two ends together in front of the arm with as many knots as you can. The more knots you can tie at this point the more impressive the trick. Obviously if you are doing this around a spectator's neck take great care!

6 It appears that the handkerchief is tied securely around the spectator's arm. Ask your audience for absolute silence – or perhaps a drumroll – as you try your experiment for the first time. When you have built up sufficient tension, grab the knotted ends and yank them forwards. The loops will fall away from behind the arm, giving the impression that the handkerchief has passed right through your volunteer. The experiment was a success!

3

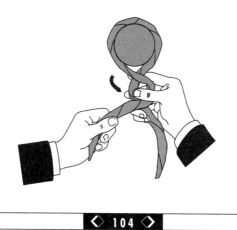

Effect *A borrowed finger ring vanishes from under a handkerchief and penetrates on to the center of a magic wand.*

Requirements *A magic wand, a fake handkerchief and a finger ring.*

Preparation *Make the magic wand from a length of dowelling rod about 30cm/12in long, and paint it black with white ends. Make the handkerchief by sewing a small pocket into one corner with the finger ring inside (illustration 1). You will need to borrow another finger ring from a member of the audience.*

• • • • • • • • • • • • • • •

1

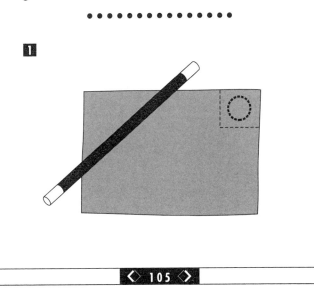

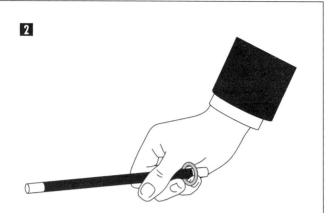

1 Introduce your magic wand to the audience by saying, "I'm a mystic and here's my stick!" Place the wand under your left arm.

2 Next you borrow a finger ring from a member of the audience. You can say, "This guarantees that at least one person will watch the rest of the trick!"

3 Using the fake handkerchief, you apparently wrap the ring up in the handkerchief. What you actually do is to move the duplicate ring, sewn inside the handkerchief, under the center of the handkerchief and grab on to it with the left hand through the layers of the cloth. Keep the borrowed ring concealed in your right hand (you do not have to palm it, just hold it in your loosely closed hand). Do not worry about it – the audience's attention will be on the handkerchief.

4 Now you remove the wand from under your left arm with your right hand. As you do this you slide the borrowed ring hidden in your right hand on to the wand (illustration 2). Practice this until you can do it smoothly and silently – the ring tends to make a noise as it hits the wand, so put in plenty of practice and you will soon get the necessary knack.

5 Tap the ring inside the handkerchief with the magic wand so that everyone can hear it is still there. Give the handkerchief to someone, and tell them to hold on to the

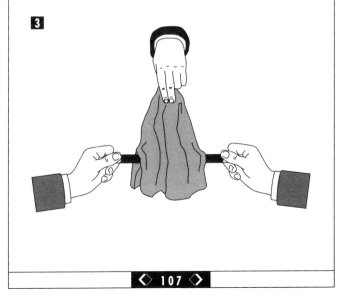

3

ring through the layers of the handkerchief. Don't give it to the ring's owner as they may be able to tell it is not their ring.

6 Hold the magic wand horizontally under the folds of the handkerchief and invite the owner of the ring to hold on to the two ends of the wand. Remove your hand. The borrowed ring on the center of the wand will be covered by the folds of the handkerchief (illustration 3).

7 Take one corner of the handkerchief and pull it sharply away from the "hanky holder's" hand. The ring appears threaded on the center of the magic wand. It seems the spectator was holding the ring until the last moment – when it suddenly returned to its rightful owner!

SIEGFRIED AND ROY

German born illusionists Siegfried and Roy are world famous for their magic with live lions, tigers, panthers and an elephant! These creatures, plus state-of-the-art special effects and their infectious enthusiasm make their live show in Las Vegas the most theatrical, dramatic and spectacular magic show in the world.

Siegfried Fishbacher and Roy Horn met on a ship cruising to New York. Roy was a bell-boy and Siegfried a passenger who did an impromptu magic show. They arrived in New York and never went back!

ENTERTAINING
ANIMATION

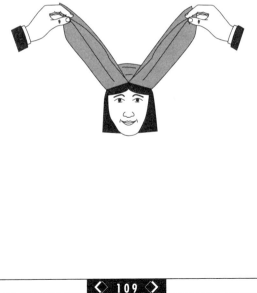

Effect *The magician transforms a white pocket handkerchief into a rabbit puppet.*

Requirements *A white cotton pocket handkerchief (about 45 x 45cm/18 x18in). This can be borrowed from a member of the audience.*

Preparation *None.*

● ● ● ● ● ● ● ● ● ● ● ● ● ● ● ●

1 Hold out your right hand, palm downwards. Drape the handkerchief over it as shown in illustration 1. About 8cm/3in of the handkerchief should hang below your fingers.

1

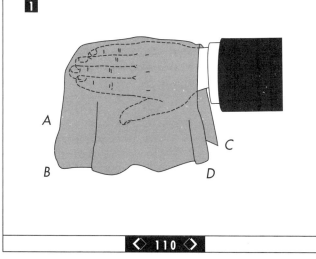

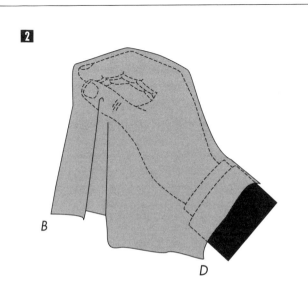

2 Bend the right fingertips inwards to touch the thumb as in illustration 2.

3 The left hand takes the front corner A which hangs down to the right and pulls it up to clip it between the right first and second fingers. The left hand then pulls up the corner B hanging down to the left, and clips it between right third and fourth fingers.

4 Pull the corners C and D up together over your wrist, wrap them around your arm and tuck the ends in.

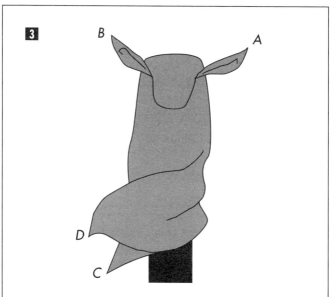

3

B

A

D

C

5 Hey presto – one magic rabbit! You can make the rabbit more lifelike by moving your fingers to make it nod, shake and wiggle (illustration 3). By moving your thumb you can even make the ears move!

TOP TIPS FOR TRICKSTERS

It is worthwhile becoming friendly with a local seamstress who will be able to make an excellent job of the various fake handkerchiefs described in this book – and well worth the modest charge.

This is more of an entertaining stunt than a magic trick, but it is an amusing "bit of business" to do between your other tricks.

Effect *The magician claims he can transform a member of the audience into a rabbit! A volunteer comes up to assist and the magician turns a handkerchief into a pair of lifelike rabbit ears. These are put on the volunteer to complete the transformation!*

Requirements *A pocket handkerchief 45 x 45cm/18 x18in. This can be borrowed from the audience.*

Preparation *None.*

● ● ● ● ● ● ● ● ● ● ● ● ● ● ● ●

1

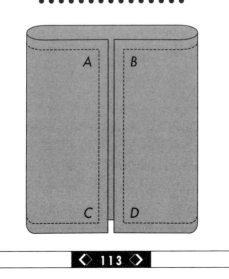

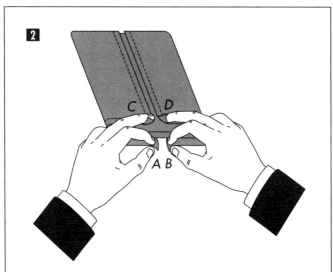

1 Lay the handkerchief flat on a table and fold the two sides to the center so that they nearly touch (illustration 1).

2 With your left hand clip the handkerchief at the point halfway down the left edge. At the same time your right hand clips the point halfway down the right edge. LIft the handkerchief up off the table top. This will fold the handkerchief in half (illustration 2).

3 Place the handkerchief back on the table. With the left hand clip the corners on the left of center (A and C) – one folded on top, one below. The right hand clips the remaining corners on the right of center (B and D) – one folded on top, one below (illustration 2).

4 Pull the hands, and corners, apart. The left hand moves to the left and the right hand moves to the right. The result is a pair of ears. You can place them on a spectator's head and claim you have changed them into a rabbit (illustration 3)!

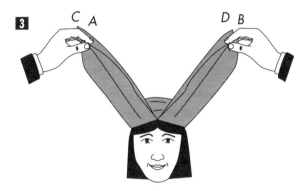

Effect *The magician spreads his pocket handkerchief flat on the table and slowly folds the four corners to the center. He grabs the air and claims to have captured a ghost. He places the invisible spook inside the handkerchief. Slowly a solid object forms inside the handkerchief. When the magician opens the handkerchief it is empty once again.*

Requirements *A gentleman's pocket handkerchief with a wide hem and a length of coat hanger wire.*

Preparation *Cut a length of coat hanger wire about 6.5cm/2.5in long. Carefully insert this into the hem of the handkerchief at one corner and sew it in place with a needle and thread. Keep this handkerchief in your pocket and you will always be ready to perform this baffling close-up effect.*

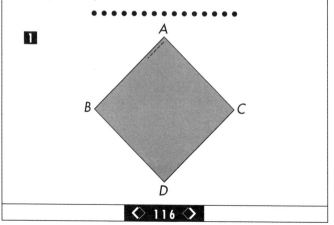

2

D

1 This is a great effect to do when the conversation at a party or social event has come around to ghosts, spirits and spooks. You can offer to try an experiment as you claim that they are floating around all the time.

2 Bring out the handkerchief and spread it out flat on the table with the "wire corner"A pointing towards the spectators and away from you (illustration 1).

3 Fold the wire corner A (the one furthest away from you) into the center of the handkerchief.

4 Fold the corner B pointing to your left into the center so that it covers the first folded corner.

5 Fold the corner C pointing to your right into the center so that the folds on both the right and left edges are even.

TOP TIPS FOR TRICKSTERS

Always have an emergency sewing kit in your "bag of tricks" when you have any hanky tricks in the act!

3

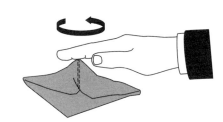

6 These three folds create a small pocket with an opening towards you (illustration 2).

7 Reach into the air with your right hand and pretend to catch one of the little ghosts floating around you. Ensure that the audience can see that your hand is really empty.

8 Your left hand lifts up the folded corners to allow you to slide your right hand into the pocket to apparently trap the ghost inside. While inside the pocket your right hand grabs the wire sewn into the hem and stands it upright on one end.

9 Remove your right hand from inside. The wire will remain standing inside and when the left hand lets go of

TOP TIPS FOR TRICKSTERS

Tricks with silk handkerchieves are not particularly suitable for outdoor shows like garden parties and fetes as they can easily be ruined by a gust of wind!

the corners it will appear that "something" has solidified inside the handkerchief. This is a very spooky illusion.

10 To prove further that it is a solid object, stretch your right hand out flat and rest it on top of the handkerchief so that the end of the wire presses against your fingers. While pressing down slightly move your hand in a small circular motion, creating the illusion of a solid round object (illustration 3).

11 Borrow a spoon from the dinner table and hit the top of the secret wire with the back of the bowl of the spoon. The sound of metal on metal is very convincing and the object sounds solid (illustration 4).

12 Return the spoon and flick open the handkerchief in an attempt to see the ghost. But the ghost is too quick for you – and you are left with two empty hands, an empty handkerchief and a freaked-out bunch of friends!

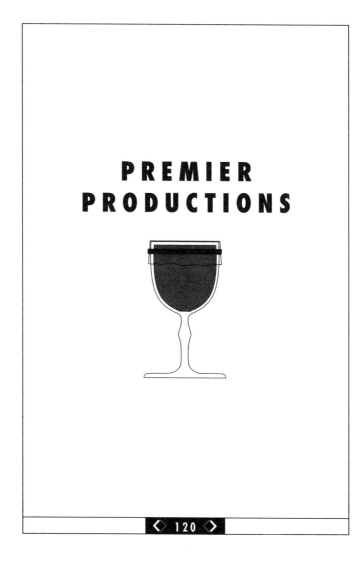

PREMIER
PRODUCTIONS

Effect *This is a flashy way to produce a silk handkerchief apparently from mid-air. The key to this effect is the special method for folding and rolling the handkerchief described below.*

Requirements *A silk handkerchief.*

Preparation *a) Place the handkerchief flat on the table in front of you with the four corners pointing north (A), south (B), east (C) and west (D).*

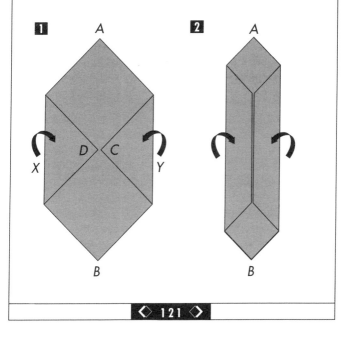

b) Fold the corners D and C into the center of the handkerchief so that they meet (illustration 1).

c) Fold the X and Y edges that you have just formed into the center so that they almost touch (illustration 2).

d) Continue folding in these parallel side edges of the handkerchief until it is about 8cm/3in wide.

e) Lastly, fold the righthand half of the handkerchief over on top of the lefthand half.

f) Fold over the bottom 2.5cm/1in of the handkerchief to the right to make a protruding tab (illustration 3).

3

g) Roll up the handkerchief from the end B with the tab so that the tab sticks out at the side. When you have rolled up the entire length of the handkerchief you will have a tight bundle (illustration 4).

B

h) Tuck the end into the bottom Z of the folded bundle. This will hold everything *rolled in place. Conceal the compact bundle somewhere behind a prop on your table or in your right pocket so that you can easily pick it up unnoticed during your performance.*

• • • • • • • • • • • • • • •

1 To perform the effect, first pick up the handkerchief secretly. Clip the tab B with your right thumb. Keep the back of your hand towards the audience so that they are unaware of the bundle (illustration 5). Do not worry about anyone seeing the bundle in your hand – if you do not draw attention to it, nobody else will notice.

4

B

Z

TOP TIPS FOR TRICKSTERS

If you do hire somebody else to make your fake handkerchief make sure that they keep the secret!

2 Turn your right side towards the audience. Reach into the air and make a grabbing motion as though you were plucking an imaginary handkerchief from mid-air. As you do this straighten out your fingers and snap your wrist. This will cause the bundle to unroll and open very quickly. Hold tightly to the corner with your right thumb. This is a startling visual appearance. It seems that the handkerchief has appeared from nowhere.

This is an ideal flourishy opener for a series of effects with a silk handkerchief.

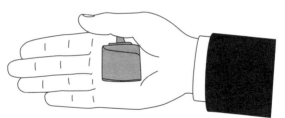

TOP TIPS FOR TRICKSTERS

A good way to prevent silk handkerchiefs looking creased is to wash them while they are tightly screwed into a ball. This will make them almost "crease proof."

Effect *This is a great opening effect. The magician shows both sides of a handkerchief. He then drapes it over his hand and a form appears underneath – it is a full glass of wine!*

Requirements *An opaque handkerchief about 60 x 60cm/24 x 24in square, a piece of cloth to match the jacket you will wear when you perform, a full wine glass and cover (see below).*

Preparation *Put the wine glass on the cloth that matches your jacket and draw around the base. Cut out the circle and stick it securely on the base. Make sure the liquid is sealed inside the glass with a cover. You can make this with a piece of cling wrapheld over the mouth of the glass with an elastic band (illustration 1). Fill the glass and seal it. Position the glass with the base*

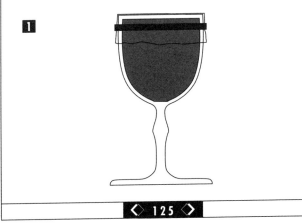

*at the front under your left armpit – the stem of the glass
runs under your armpit. Because of the extra piece of
material on the base of the glass it is camouflaged
against your jacket. Now you see why this has to be
your opening effect! Drape the handkerchief over your
left arm and you are ready to amaze your audience.*

● ● ● ● ● ● ● ● ● ● ● ● ● ● ● ●

1 Both hands hold the handkerchief at the corners of the
top edge. The thumbs grip over the hem with the fingers
concealed behind the handkerchief (illustration 2).

2 Turn the handkerchief around to show there is nothing
on the other side. You do this by crossing your arms.

Your right hand moves behind your left arm. Your left hand moves to the right to stop in front of your right elbow (illustration 3).

3 In this position your right fingers clip the stem of the wineglass. When the fingers are gripping the base relax your pressure with your left arm and the glass will swing upside down out of sight behind the handkerchief. This all happens as you are apparently just displaying the handkerchief.

4 Move your hands back to their original positions. The upside down glass is kept concealed behind the handkerchief, with the right fingers clipping the stem (illustration 4).

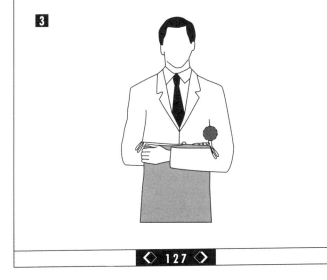

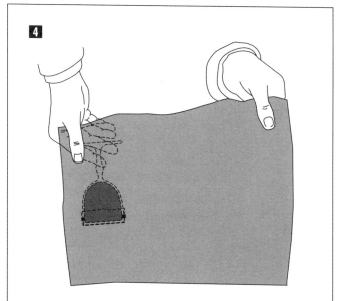

5 The right thumb releases its hold on the corner of the handkerchief and the right hand, with the glass clipped between its fingers, slides under the handkerchief to the approximate center. It seems that the handkerchief covers your empty right hand. The glass is concealed in the drapes of the handkerchief.

6 The left hand lets go of its corner and pulls straight up on the center of the handkerchief. As you do this be careful you do not pull too far otherwise the glass will be revealed hanging from the right hand.

7 The right fingers curl into the palm of your hand bringing the glass up with them. The left hand releases its hold on the center of the handkerchief and it falls over the glass. To the audience it seems impossible for anything to have appeared under the handkerchief.

8 The left fingers take hold of the center of the handkerchief and, through the fabric, remove the cover on the mouth of the glass as they pull up the handkerchief to reveal a full glass of wine (illustration 5). The cover is taken away in the handkerchief and both are discarded to one side. Give the drink to a member of your audience to confirm it is real, and joke that "all my tricks look better when you've had a drink!"

5

Effect *After showing both sides of a newspaper the magician punches holes in it – through which he then produces an apparently endless stream of silk handkerchiefs.*

Requirements *A sheet of newspaper, silk handkerchiefs, a matchbox cover, adhesive tape and a strip of thin metal.*

Preparation *You need to make a special prop to contain the handkerchiefs. Take the matchbox cover and seal up one end of it with adhesive tape. Then load as many handkerchiefs inside as you can. It is amazing how many silk handkerchiefs will compress into such a small space.*

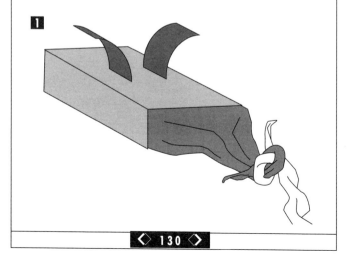

Attach the thin strip of metal to the matchbox cover with adhesive tape (illustration 1). Bend the metal as shown, so that it can be clipped behind your fingers when your hand is open flat.

Clip the box in position on the back of your right hand.

• • • • • • • • • • • • • • • •

1 Hold the newspaper in your right hand with your fingers behind it, as in illustration 2.

2 Take the bottom edge of the newspaper with the left hand. Fold it up to the right hand. As you do so, the right hand releases its grip on the top edge. Keep the right hand held out straight so that the fingers conceal

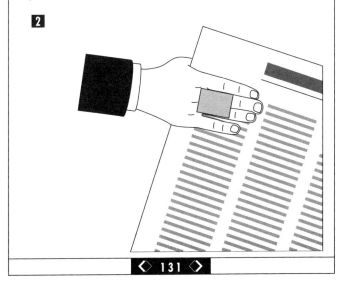

the box from the audience. The audience now see the other side of the newspaper and the apparently empty right hand.

3 You can say to the audience, "Everybody says that there is nothing in the newspapers these days, but it is just not true. They are always full of leaflets and vouchers and special offers that are folded inside. I wonder what we'll find hidden inside this one?"

4 Move your right hand down the edge of the newspaper so that it is nearer the center. With the left hand punch a hole in the newspaper. Reach through the hole with the left fingers and at the same time bend the right fingers so that the open end of the box meets the left fingers. The left fingers pull the first handkerchief out through the hole in the newspaper (illustration 3).

5 The right hand returns to the top edge of the newspaper and the left hand turns the newspaper again as described in step 2.

6 Punch another hole in the newspaper and produce another handkerchief, as described in step 4.

7 Repeat this procedure until all the handkerchiefs have been produced.

8 When the box is empty, bend the right fingers forward so the box is resting against the back of the paper. Wrap the newspaper around the box and discard it. You are left with two empty hands and pile of silk handkerchiefs, perhaps for use in your next effect.

This makes an ideal opening effect for a routine of handkerchief magic because you are able to produce all the handkerchiefs you will need.

TOP TIPS FOR TRICKSTERS

When doing any effects which rely on having something hidden inside the layers of the handkerchief (coins, matches, etc.) always ensure that you do not have a direct light source behind you!

Effect *The magician shows two square tubes to be empty. The audience can see both tubes empty at the same time. It seems that nothing could be concealed inside. Yet the magician reaches inside and produces a large number of silk handkerchiefs, ribbons and maybe props for the next effect!*

Requirements *Two square tubes which nest one inside the other, a small box which will fit inside the nested tubes and silk handkerchiefs, ribbons and anything else that you wish to produce.*

1

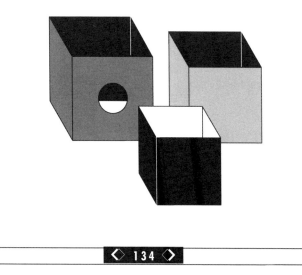

Preparation *Cut a small hole in the front of the larger tube and paint the interior of both boxes with a matt black paint. Paint the small box with the same black paint. Cover the outside of the two tubes with a colorful design (illustration 1). Fill the black box with your items to be produced. Depending on the size of this production box you could produce handkerchiefs, ribbons, sweets, soft toys or full glasses for your audience.*

Load the black box inside the two nested tubes and place them on your table with the hole in the large tube facing the audience.

● ● ● ● ● ● ● ● ● ● ● ● ● ● ● ● ●

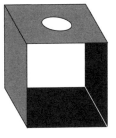 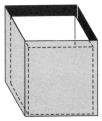

TOP TIPS FOR TRICKSTERS

The most important rule of all – before you begin any performance always check your flies!

1 Lift up the outer tube and hold it up the audience to show it is empty (illustration 2). Place it back in position around the inner tube.

2 Lift up the inner tube. This can be held up and shown to be empty (illustration 3). The audience can also see through the hole in the large tube, but because the production box has been painted black they will believe they are seeing the back of the outer tube. This clever principle is known among magicians as "black art".

3 Replace the inner tube inside the larger tube.

4 After sufficient build-up, roll up your sleeves, show both your hands are empty and make your production

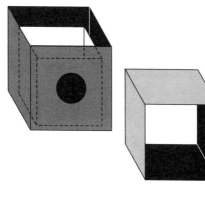

RESTORATIONS

Effect *A match is wrapped in the folds of a handkerchief and a member of the audience snaps it into several pieces. The magician unfolds the handkerchief to show the match is restored and is completely undamaged.*

Requirements *A pocket handkerchief with a wide hem and a box of matches.*

Preparation *Take one of the matches and slide it into the open end of the hem (illustration 1). Push it inside until it is concealed from view.*

• • • • • • • • • • • • • •

1

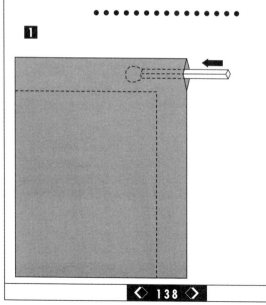

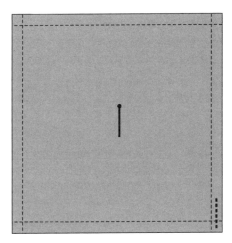

1 Bring out the box of matches and open them. Ask a member of the audience to "pick a match, any match!" and take it out of the box.

2 Bring out the handkerchief and spread it out flat on the table. Ensure that the corner with the match in it is nearest you.

3 Ask the spectator to place their freely selected match in the middle of the handkerchief (illustration 2).

4 Fold the "hidden match corner" over the selected match (illustration 3). Next fold the diagonally opposite corner over on top, followed by the last two corners.

5 Now feel through the folds of the handkerchief for the secret match. The selected match will remain hidden inside the folds of the handkerchief.

6 Hand the match, wrapped in the folds of the handkerchief, to the spectator and tell them to break the match several times (illustration 4). They believe they are breaking their selected match, but in fact they break the secret match which is hidden in the hem.

7 When the spectator is convinced the match has been completely destroyed, slowly and dramatically unfold the corners of the handkerchief. The audience will be amazed to see that the broken match has now completely restored.

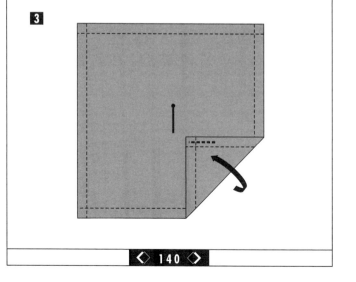

Hand the match out for examination, and take the opportunity to stuff the handkerchief in your pocket!

4

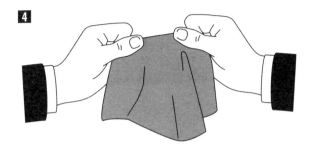

MASKELYNE (1839-1917)
AND DEVANT (1868-1941)

In the early 1900s John Nevil Maskelyne and David Devant were England's most famous magicians running "England's Home of Mystery" firstly at the Egyptian Hall and later at St George's Hall in London.

Devant was a charming gentleman on stage (his publicity proclaimed "All Done By Kindness"), while Maskelyne was an acclaimed inventor and creator. Among Maskelyne's inventions was Psycho, a card-playing, mind-reading automaton. Together the two magicians were an unbeatable team and their sell-out shows were a "must" on any trip to London at the turn of the century.

◇ CUT AND RESTORED HANKY ◇

Effect *The magician holds a silk handkerchief which is cut in half by a member of the audience. The magician folds the handkerchief into a tight bundle and in full view of the audience the handkerchief is restored!*

Requirements *A silk handkerchief about 45 x 45cm/ 18 x 18in and a pair of sharp scissors.*

Preparation *None.*

● ● ● ● ● ● ● ● ● ● ● ● ● ● ● ●

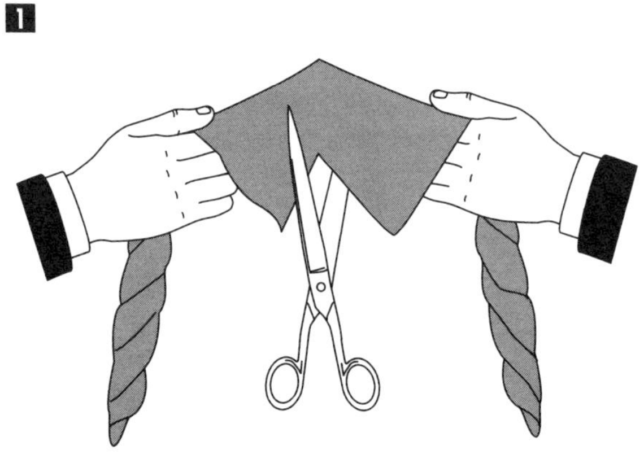

1

1 Hold the handkerchief by two diagonally opposite corners and twist it to form it into a rope.

2 With your thumbs, separate the two corners which are in the center of the handkerchief so that one points towards you and one points towards the spectator. Do this before the handkerchief is cut.

3 Hand the scissors to a member of your audience. Hold your hands either side of the center section to prevent the rope from untwisting. Ask the spectator to

---

TOP TIPS FOR TRICKSTERS

Always have your own clean handkerchief on hand when doing any tricks that require one borrowed from the audience, just in case none are in a fit state for public display!

cut through the center of the handkerchief (illustration 1). Warn them not to cut off your fingers! If your career as a magician is going to be successful you'll need to hang on to them!

Warning The spectator really does cut through the handkerchief, so every time that you perform this effect a handkerchief will be cut in half! It needs to be a good trick to be worth the expense – and it is!

4 After the spectator has finished cutting through the handkerchief separate your hands to show that it really has been cut into two equal pieces (illustration 2).

5 Say, "Does anybody have a needle and thread? No? It's okay, I'm only kidding. I'm a magician so I can fix this back together with magic."

6 Place the two halves on top of each other (illustration 3) so that two cut edges are on top of each other.

7 Hold the silks in one hand at the top and with the other hand twist the two dangling "ropes" around the center. As you do this make sure that the four cut corners are sticking out, two on either side (illustration 4).

8 Grab the two corners sticking out on the left with your left first finger and thumb and those sticking out on the right with your right first finger and thumb and slowly pull your hands apart (illustration 4).

Pull   Pull

9 An amazing visual effect will occur as the handkerchief unfolds revealing an apparently restored handkerchief (illustration 5). If you keep the handkerchief pulled tight between your hands, the cut along the center will be hidden. This really is a very stunning effect and well worth the expense!

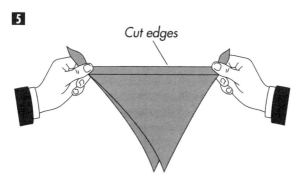

5

Cut edges

SILKEN SORCERY CLASSICS

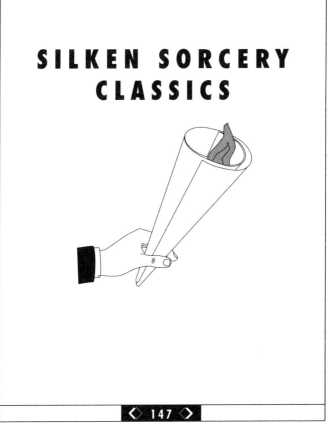

Effect *Two silk handkerchiefs are tied together and put on one side. A third silk handkerchief vanishes and re-appears in an impossible place – tied between the other two!*

Requirements *Four silk handkerchiefs – two of a matching plain color (red) and two matching multi-colored ones. It is important that a corner of the multi-colored handkerchiefs matches the plain red ones.*

Preparation *Prepare one of the plain red handker-chiefs by folding it in half diagonally and sewing the two halves together about 4cm/1.5in away from the folded edge (illustration 1). Use sewing thread the same color as the silk so that the secret preparation will not be visible to the audience. Tie corner D of the prepared red silk to the corner of the multi-colored silk that is diago-nally opposite its matching red corner (illustration 1). Starting at the tied end, push the multi-colored silk into the secret pocket in the prepared handkerchief until only the red corner sticks out (illustration 2). It should appear that this is the corner of the red handkerchief.*

1 Display the two red handkerchiefs and apparently tie them together. In fact you tie the corner of the genuine red handkerchief to the corner of the multi-colored silk hidden in the secret pocket. Now place the tied handkerchiefs somewhere on view. You can place them

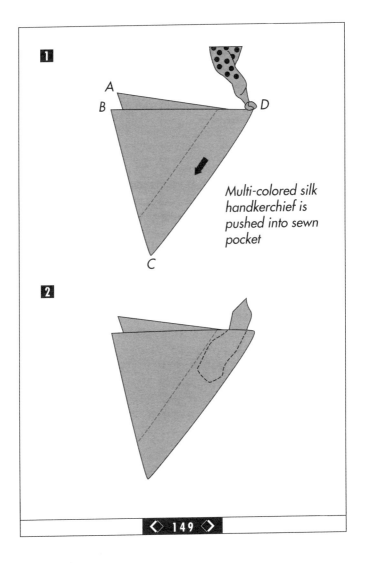

1

A
B
D
C

Multi-colored silk handkerchief is pushed into sewn pocket

2

inside an empty tumbler or glass – or invite a member of the audience to hold the handkerchiefs balled up between their hands. That way there is no way you can get at them.

2 Vanish the duplicate multi-colored silk handkerchief. You could use the "Paper Bag Vanish" or "Vanish in Newspaper."

3 Grab one corner of the two tied handkerchiefs and pull them out sharply. This pulls the hidden multi-colored handkerchief from the secret pocket, and the audience see the handkerchief which apparently vanished just seconds before is now tied between the two red silk handkerchiefs (illustration 3).

If you invited a member of the audience up to hold on to the tied handkerchiefs you could say that they will never be trusted by their friends again!

3

Effect *A newspaper is folded into a cone and a handkerchief is tucked inside. When the newspaper is unfolded the handkerchief has gone!*

Requirements *A silk handkerchief, a newspaper and some glue.*

Preparation *You need to make a secret pocket in the newspaper. This is done by taking a double-page spread and gluing it together along three of the four edges so that the top is left open (illustration 1). When you have done this you will be left with a paper bag made from a newspaper.*

• • • • • • • • • • • • • • • •

1

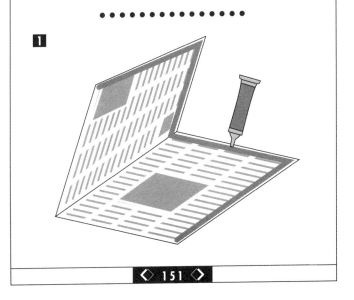

1 Show the sheet of newspaper on both sides.

2 Roll the newspaper into a cone with the opening to the secret pocket at the top.

3 Pretend to put the handkerchief into the cone, but really insert it between the layers of the newspaper in the secret pocket (illustration 2).

4 Open up the cone to show that the handkerchief has completely disappeared!

5 You can finish by saying, "There never is anything in the newspaper these days!"

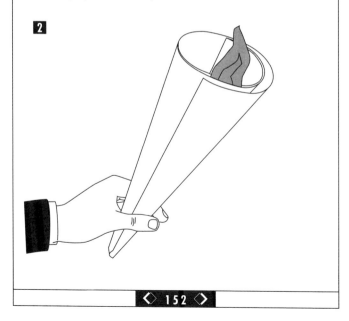

2

Effect *Six large silk handkerchiefs are shown. Three are put on one side while the remaining three are tied together. Acting in sympathy, the first set become tied together. After untying this set of three handkerchiefs it is discovered that the original "tied trio" have untied too! As a big finish the magician throws all six handkerchiefs into the air where they tie themselves together!*

Requirements *A large elastic band (to match your skin color), six large silk handkerchiefs (each about 75 x 75cm/30 x 30in) and a chair.*

1

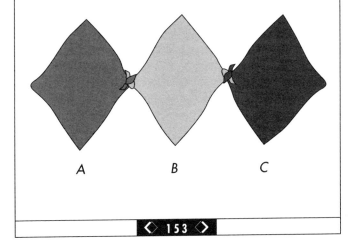

A   B   C

Preparation *Tie three of the contrasting colored handkerchiefs together by the corners to form a chain (illustration 1). We will call these A, B and C. Drape these handkerchiefs over the back of the chair so that they appear unconnected. This is done by draping three untied corners over the front of the chair. The knots are hidden behind the back of the chair. Drape the three loose handkerchiefs (D, E and F) over the back of the chair alongside A, B and C (illustration 2). Finally place the elastic band over the little finger of your left hand.*

• • • • • • • • • • • • • • • • •

1 Pick up D and hold its top corner between the thumb and first finger of your left hand. Pick up A, B and C

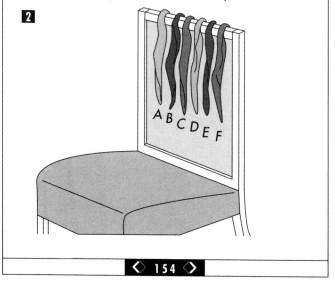

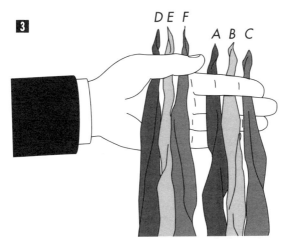

3

D E F   A B C

together by the three untied corners and place these corners between the left first and second fingers. The knots will remain hidden in the folds of the handker-chiefs. Finally E and F are picked up and held between the left thumb and first finger, as far as possible from the first silk (illustration 3). It should appear to the audience that you are just picking up the handkerchiefs and that nothing untoward is happening. For this to be the case it is essential that you rehearse this initial preparation as much as the actual trick.

2 This set-up has prepared you to do a special false count. This false count will enable you to show that all of the silk handkerchiefs are separate – even though they are not.

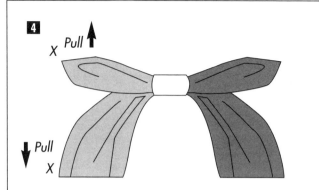

a) Hold both hands in front of you and with the right hand take the first loose silk (F) from between the left thumb and first finger and hold it up to the right saying "one."

b) Bring the right hand back to the left and remove silk E as you say "two."

c) Again bring both hands together, apparently to take another single silk, but what you actually do is replace E and F between the left thumb and first finger and take A, B and C from between the right first and second finger. As you do this say "three." If done well – and this must be practiced until you can do it well – this first count should appear to be identical to the first two.

d) Count D, E and F from your left hand into your right hand one at a time saying "four, five and six."

3 Take A, B and C and drop them on the seat of the chair saying "three separate handkerchiefs" making use of that great magician's tool known as lying through your teeth!

4 Tie the corners of D, E and F together with two reef knots (see Glossary) to form a chain of three handkerchiefs. Do not tie the knots too tightly as in a moment you will have to secretly untie them! You do this by pulling on one silk either side of the knot (illustration 4), apparently to tighten it. This converts the reef knot into a slip knot. Repeat this with the second knot.

5 Hold a knot in the palm of each hand (illustration 5) and close your hands around the knots. As you do this

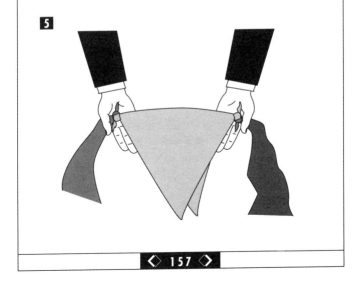

your fingers hold on to the center silk, while the thumbs and first fingers pull on the silks on either end to slide them free of the knots. You do all this as you apparently bundle up the silks into one hand. With the other hand lift up A, B and C from the chair and show they have miraculously joined together, apparently in sympathy with the others D, E and F.

6 Place on the seat of the chair the now separate D, E and F (the audience believe these are still tied together) as you say "three knotted handkerchiefs." Now untie A, B and C.

7 As you are untying the knots move the elastic band from around your left little finger and stretch it over all the fingers and thumb of the left hand. As each handkerchief is untied tuck a corner inside the stretched elastic band.

8 Now pick up D, E and F from the chair to show that they too are untied. As each handkerchief in turn is shown separately it is added to the silks in the left hand and a corner secretly tucked into the elastic band.

9 Offer to prove that the handkerchiefs are truly sympathetic silks. Throw them all into the air. It appears that in mid-air they all become knotted together. Of course it is really the elastic band holding them together and they were all connected before you threw them! This is a convincing illusion and a great ending to a classic piece of silken sorcery!